MW01259685

Purpose   This course provides training on and resources for personnel who require a basic understanding of the National Incident Management System (NIMS).

Course Objective   The course objective is to enable participants to demonstrate basic knowledge of NIMS.

Training Content   The training is comprised of the following units:

- Unit 1: Course Overview
- Unit 2: Understanding NIMS
- Unit 3: NIMS Preparedness
- Unit 4: NIMS Communications and Information Management
- Unit 5: NIMS Resource Management
- Unit 6: NIMS Command and Management
- Unit 7: Additional Resources and Course Summary

UNIT 1: COURSE OVERVIEW

Objectives

At the end of this unit, you should be able to describe the purpose of the course.

Scope

- Unit Introduction
- Course Objectives
- Participant Introductions
- Expectations: Participant and Instructor
- Course Logistics
- Successful Course Completion
- NIMS Document Orientation

Your Notes:

Unit Introduction and Course Objectives

Image 1.1

Key Points

This course will introduce you to the National Incident Management System (NIMS).

This course provides a basic introduction to NIMS. It is not designed to replace Incident Command System and position-specific training.

Image 1.2

Course Objectives

Describe:

- The intent of NIMS.
- The key concepts and principles underlying NIMS.
- The purpose of the NIMS components.
- The purpose of the National Integration Center (NIC).

National Incident Management System, An Introduction
IS-0700.A – October 2014
Visual 1.2

Key Points

At the end of this course, you will be able to:

- Describe the intent of NIMS.
- Describe the key concepts and principles underlying NIMS.
- Describe the purpose of the NIMS components including:
    - Preparedness
    - Communications and Information Management
    - Resource Management
    - Command and Management
- Describe the purpose of the National Integration Center (NIC).

Image 1.3

Participant Introductions

- Name, job title, and organization
- Overall experience with emergency or incident response

National Incident Management System, An Introduction
IS-0700.A – October 2014
Visual 1.3

Key Points

Introduce yourself by providing:

- Your name, job titles, and organization.
- Your overall experience with emergency or incident response.

Introduction and Expectations

Image 1.4

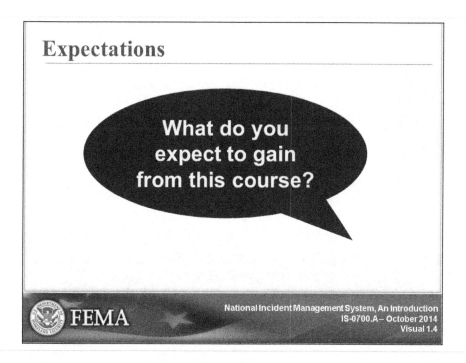

Key Points

Answer the following question:

What do you expect to gain from this course?

Image 1.5

Instructor Expectations

- Cooperate with the group.
- Be open minded to new ideas.
- Participate actively in all of the training activities and exercises.
- Return to class at the stated time.

National Incident Management System, An Introduction
IS-0700.A – October 2014
Visual 1.5

Key Points

Your instructor expects that you will:

- Cooperate with the group.
- Be open minded to new ideas.
- Participate actively in all of the training activities and exercises.
- Return to class at the stated time.

Course Logistics and Successful Course Completion

Image 1.6

Key Points

Your instructor will review the following information:

- Course agenda
- Sign-in sheet

Your instructor will review the following housekeeping issues:

- Breaks
- Message and telephone location
- Cell phone policy
- Facilities
- Other concerns

Image 1.7

Successful Course Completion

- Participate in unit activities/exercises.
- Achieve 75% or higher on the final exam.
- Complete the end-of-course evaluation.

FEMA

National Incident Management System, An Introduction
IS-0700.A – October 2014
Visual 1.7

Key Points

In order to successfully complete this course, you must:

- Participate in unit activities/exercises.
- Achieve 75% or higher on the final exam.
- Complete the end-of-course evaluation.

The next unit will provide an overview of the National Incident Management System.

NIMS Document Orientation

Image 1.8

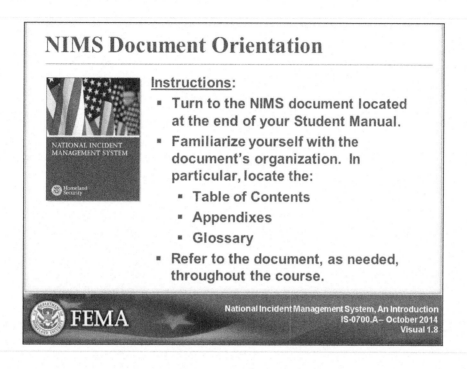

Key Points

Spend a few moments looking through the NIMS document to become familiar with its organization. Each unit in this course corresponds to certain segments of the NIMS document.

Refer to the NIMS document and its glossary, as needed, throughout the course.

UNIT 2: UNDERSTANDING NIMS

Objectives

At the end of this unit, you should be able to describe:

- The intent of NIMS.
- Key concepts and principles underlying NIMS.

Scope

- Unit Introduction
- Introduction to NIMS.
    - Video: What is NIMS?
    - NIMS Overview
    - What NIMS Is/What It's Not
    - Mandates
    - Collaborative Incident Management
    - NIMS Builds on Best Practices
    - Flexibility
    - Standardization
    - Voices of Experience
    - NIMS Components
- Knowledge Review and Summary

Unit Introduction and Objectives

Image 2.1

Key Points

Unit 2 provides a general overview of the National Incident Management System, or NIMS. The next visual will outline the objectives for this unit.

Image 2.2

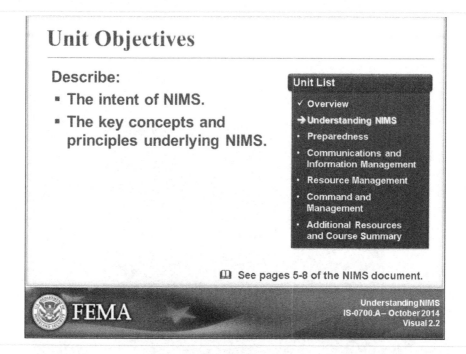

Key Points

This lesson summarizes the information presented in the Introduction and Overview of the NIMS document, including:

- Introduction
- Concepts and Principles
- Flexibility
- Standardization
- Overview of NIMS Components

Refer to pages 5 through 8 of the NIMS document.

Introduction to NIMS

Image 2.3

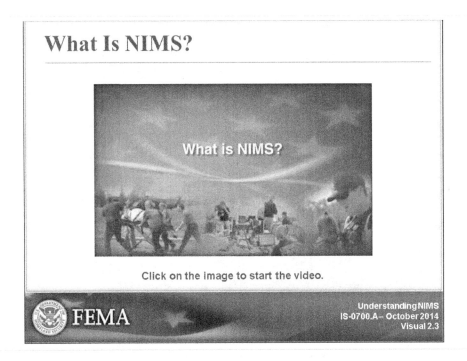

Key Points

The video provides an introduction to NIMS.

Video Transcript: Each day communities respond to numerous emergencies. Most often, these incidents are managed effectively at the local level.

However, there are some incidents that may require a collaborative approach that includes personnel from:

- Multiple jurisdictions,
- A combination of specialties or disciplines,
- Several levels of government,
- Nongovernmental organizations, and
- The private sector.

The National Incident Management System, or NIMS, provides the foundation needed to ensure that we can work together when our communities and the Nation need us the most.

NIMS integrates best practices into a comprehensive, standardized framework that is flexible enough to be applicable across the full spectrum of potential incidents, regardless of cause, size, location, or complexity.

Using NIMS allows us to work together to prepare for, prevent, respond to, recover from, and mitigate the effects of incidents. This course introduces you to the NIMS concepts, principles, and components.

Image 2.4

NIMS Overview

What ? . . . NIMS provides a consistent nationwide template . . .

Who? . . . to enable Federal, State, tribal, and local governments, the private sector, and nongovernmental organizations to work together . . .

How? . . . to prepare for, prevent, respond to, recover from, and mitigate the effects of incidents regardless of cause, size, location, or complexity . . .

Why? . . . in order to reduce the loss of life and property, and harm to the environment.

 FEMA

Understanding NIMS
IS-0700.A – October 2014
Visual 2.4

Key Points

The **National Incident Management System (NIMS) provides a consistent framework for incident management at all jurisdictional levels regardless of the cause, size, or complexity of the incident**. NIMS is not an operational incident management or resource allocation plan.

The NIMS document was developed through a collaborative intergovernmental partnership with significant input from the incident management functional disciplines, nongovernmental organizations (NGOs), and the private sector.

Originally published on March 1, 2004, the NIMS document was revised in 2008 to reflect contributions from stakeholders and lessons learned during recent incidents.

Image 2.5

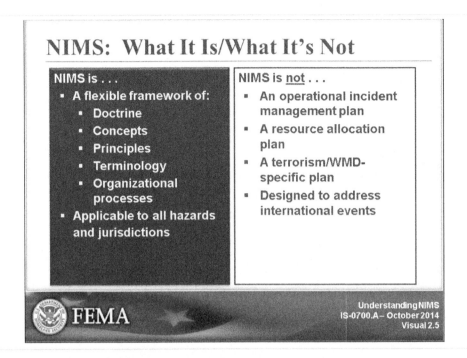

Key Points

Refer to the items on the visual stating "What NIMS Is" and "What NIMS Is Not." Read the following situations and indicate if they are consistent or inconsistent with NIMS:

- Local officials are using the Incident Command System (ICS) to plan for the upcoming Fourth of July celebration.
  Answer:

- A jurisdiction/agency follows NIMS only when incidents are complex enough to involve other jurisdictions.
  Answer:

- An agency is replacing its operational plan for responding to incidents with the guidance provided in NIMS.
  Answer:

- An organization is reorganizing and using NIMS/ICS titles for day-to-day routine activities.
  Answer:

Image 2.6

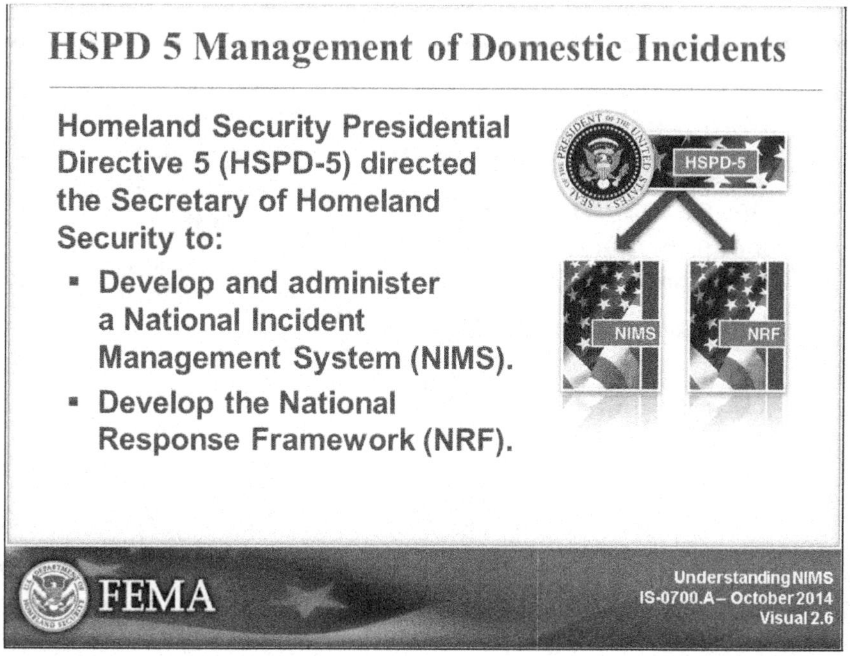

HSPD 5 Management of Domestic Incidents

Homeland Security Presidential Directive 5 (HSPD-5) directed the Secretary of Homeland Security to:

- **Develop and administer a National Incident Management System (NIMS).**
- **Develop the National Response Framework (NRF).**

FEMA

Understanding NIMS
IS-0700.A – October 2014
Visual 2.6

Key Points

Homeland Security Presidential Directive 5 (HSPD-5), "Management of Domestic Incidents," directed the Secretary of Homeland Security to:

- Develop and administer a National Incident Management System (NIMS).
- Develop the National Response Framework (NRF).

Image 2.7

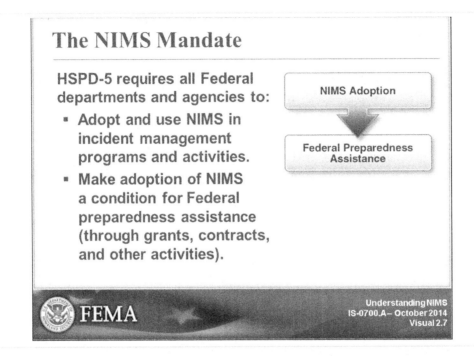

Key Points

HSPD-5 requires all Federal departments and agencies to:

- Adopt NIMS and use it in their individual incident management programs and activities.
- Make adoption of NIMS by State, tribal, and local organizations a condition for Federal preparedness assistance (through grants, contracts, and other activities).

Image 2.8

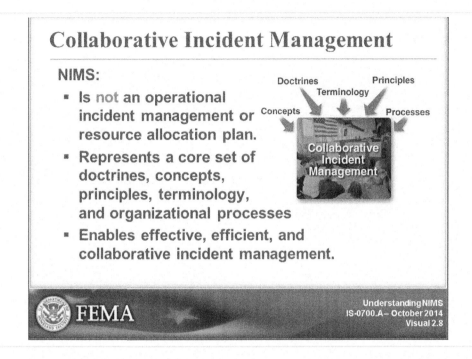

Key Points

NIMS is not an operational incident management or resource allocation plan.

NIMS represents a core set of doctrines, concepts, principles, terminology, and organizational processes that enables effective, efficient, and collaborative incident management.

Image 2.9

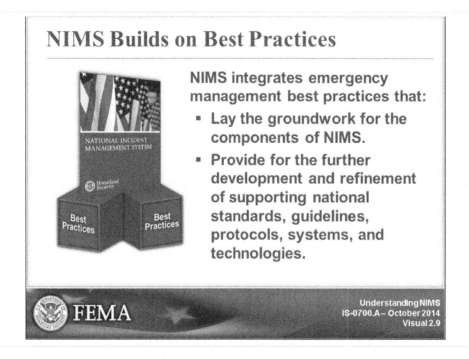

Key Points

By building on the foundation provided by existing emergency management and incident response systems used by jurisdictions, organizations, and functional disciplines at all levels, NIMS integrates best practices into a comprehensive framework.

These best practices lay the groundwork for the components of NIMS and provide the mechanisms for the further development and refinement of supporting national standards, guidelines, protocols, systems, and technologies.

Image 2.10

NIMS Is Dynamic

NIMS:

- Is not a static system.
- Fosters the development of specialized technologies that facilitate response.
- Allows for the adoption of new approaches that will enable continuous refinement of the system.

 FEMA

Understanding NIMS
IS-0700.A– October 2014
Visual 2.10

Key Points

Note that NIMS is not a static system.

NIMS fosters the development of specialized technologies that facilitate emergency management and incident response activities, and allows for the adoption of new approaches that will enable continuous refinement of the system over time.

Image 2.11

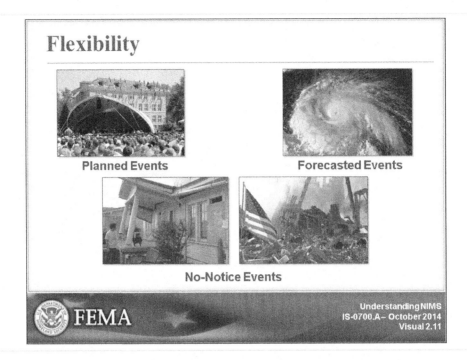

Key Points

The components of NIMS are adaptable and scalable to any situation, from routine, local incidents, to incidents requiring the activation of interstate mutual aid, to those requiring a coordinated Federal response. NIMS applies to all types of incidents.

Image 2.12

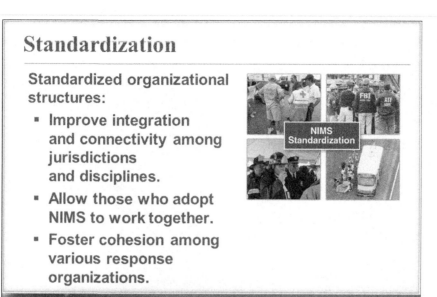

Key Points

NIMS provides a set of standardized organizational structures that improve integration and connectivity among jurisdictions and disciplines, starting with a common foundation of preparedness and planning.

Personnel and organizations that have adopted the common NIMS framework are able to work together, thereby fostering cohesion among the various organizations involved in all aspects of an incident.

Image 2.13

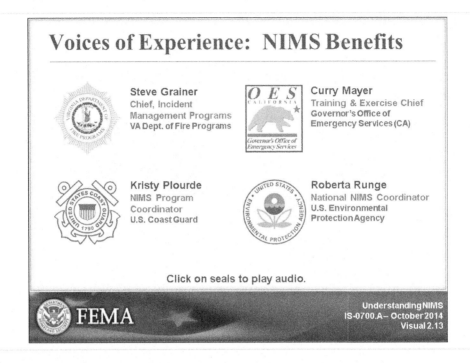

Key Points

Listen as your instructor plays audio clips about the advantages of using NIMS.

Steve Grainer, Chief, Incident Management Programs, VA Dept. of Fire Programs: NIMS is a national initiative to standardize the fundamental processes that are necessary for effectively managing significant emergencies, and it's applicable in all size and scale and scope emergencies. Having been involved at the local, State, and Federal level in a number of different venues during my career, I'm truly and honestly pleased to say that this is an opportunity for us all to better establish a baseline of competencies for not only emergencies, obviously that would be the primary focus, but also to utilize a nationally vetted process that will work given A) participation and B) commitment. So I'm all for the idea of establishing a national systems approach as is pretty much formatted through the concepts of NIMS in their entirety. It's a good thing, that's about the best I can say.

Curry Mayer, Training & Exercise Chief, Governor's Office of Emergency Services (CA): NIMS is the national structure that includes roles and responsibilities for responding to an incident that would require the Federal Government to be involved, a catastrophic or large-scale incident. It's also a system that provides common terminology, roles, and responsibilities so that everyone in the country can basically plug into the national system of response.

Kristy Plourde, NIMS Program Coordinator, U.S. Coast Guard: NIMS has helped us be better structured, have less duplication, be more organized and more efficient, and it covers the whole gambit of organization, communications, preparedness, it's the whole, it's everything.

Roberta Runge, National NIMS Coordinator, U.S. Environmental Protection Agency: NIMS is a system that allows us to plan and prepare and execute a response more effectively with our response partners. The biggest benefit to us as an agency is to be able to understand how our response partners are also going to be executing the response. EPA is a fairly large organization but we hardly ever respond to something very large and very complicated without other Federal and State and local partners. If everyone is operating the response using different terminology or a different management structure, it becomes very difficult, very fast.

Image 2.14

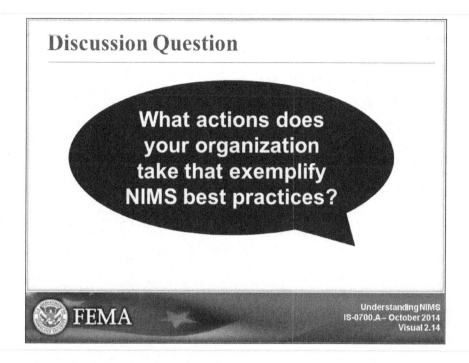

Key Points

Answer following discussion question:

- What actions does your organization take that exemplify NIMS best practices?

Image 2.15

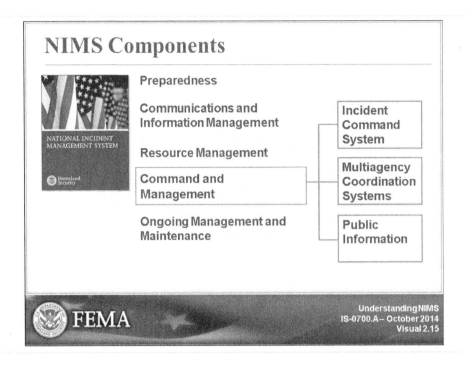

Key Points

NIMS is much more than just using the Incident Command System or an organization chart.

Following is a synopsis of each major component of NIMS.

- **Preparedness.** Effective incident management and incident response activities begin with a host of preparedness activities conducted on an ongoing basis, in advance of any potential incident. Preparedness involves an integrated combination of planning, procedures and protocols, training and exercises, personnel qualification and certification, and equipment certification.
- **Communications and Information Management.** Emergency management and incident response activities rely on communications and information systems that provide a common operating picture to all command and coordination sites. NIMS describes the requirements necessary for a standardized framework for communications and emphasizes the need for a common operating picture. NIMS is based on the concepts of interoperability, reliability, scalability, portability, and the resiliency and redundancy of communications and information systems.
- **Resource Management.** Resources (such as personnel, equipment, and/or supplies) are needed to support critical incident objectives. The flow of resources must be fluid and adaptable to the requirements of the incident. NIMS defines standardized mechanisms and establishes the resource management process to: identify requirements for, order and acquire, mobilize, track and report, recover and demobilize, reimburse for, and inventory resources.
- **Command and Management.** The Command and Management component within NIMS is designed to enable effective and efficient incident management and coordination by providing flexible, standardized incident management structures. The structure is based on three key organizational constructs: the Incident Command System, Multiagency Coordination Systems, and Public Information.
- **Ongoing Management and Maintenance.** DHS/FEMA manages the development and maintenance of NIMS. This includes developing NIMS programs and processes as well as keeping the NIMS document current.

Knowledge Review and Summary

Image 2.16

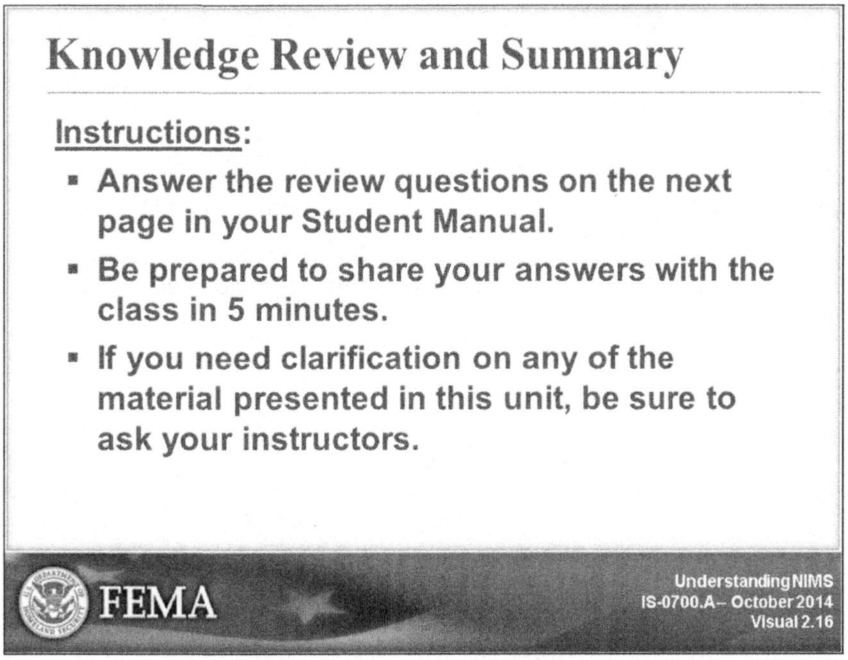

Knowledge Review and Summary

Instructions:

- Answer the review questions on the next page in your Student Manual.
- Be prepared to share your answers with the class in 5 minutes.
- If you need clarification on any of the material presented in this unit, be sure to ask your instructors.

 FEMA

Understanding NIMS
IS-0700.A – October 2014
Visual 2.16

Key Points

Instructions:

- Answer the review questions on the next page.
- Be prepared to share your answers with the class in 5 minutes.
- If you need clarification on any of the material presented in this unit, ask your instructors.

Unit 2: Knowledge Review

1. Indicate if the following statements are TRUE or FALSE:

Statement	True	False
NIMS is an operational incident management plan.	☐	☐
NIMS is based on best practices collected from all levels of responders.	☐	☐
NIMS integrates best practices into a comprehensive, standardized framework.	☐	☐
NIMS provides a terrorism/WMD-specific plan for Federal, State, tribal, and local responders.	☐	☐
NIMS is applicable across the full spectrum of potential incidents, regardless of cause, size, location, or complexity.	☐	☐
NIMS specifies how Federal and interstate mutual-aid resources will be allocated among jurisdictions.	☐	☐

2. Describe one benefit of NIMS.

3. Use the space below to make note of any questions you have about the material covered in this unit.

UNIT 3: NIMS PREPAREDNESS

Objectives

At the end of this unit, you should be able to:

- Describe the importance of preparedness.
- Identify the NIMS mechanisms and tools used to help enhance preparedness.

Scope

- Unit Introduction and Objectives
- Introduction to NIMS Preparedness
  - Video: What is NIMS Preparedness?
  - NIMS and Other Preparedness Efforts
  - NIMS and the National Response Framework
  - Elected and Appointed Officials
  - Preparedness: Continuous Cycle
  - Preparedness: A Unified Approach
  - Levels of Capability
- Preparedness Mechanisms
  - Coordination of Preparedness Activities
  - NIMS Preparedness Efforts
  - Continuity Capability
  - Mutual Aid and Assistance Agreements
- Preparedness Tools
  - Procedural Documents
  - Protocols
  - Training
  - Exercises
  - Personnel Qualifications and Certification
  - Equipment Certification
  - Mitigation and Preparedness
- Knowledge Review and Summary
- Preparedness Self-Assessment

Unit Introduction and Objectives

Image 3.1

Key Points

This lesson presents an overview of the NIMS Preparedness component.

Image 3.2

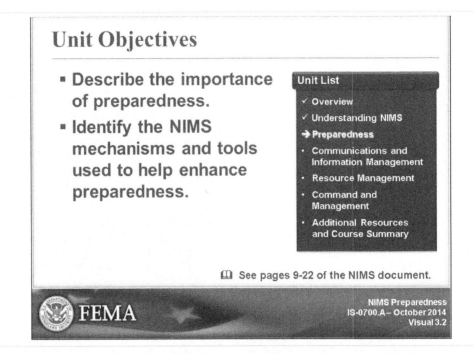

Key Points

At the end of this lesson, you should be able to:

- Describe the importance of preparedness.
- Identify the NIMS mechanisms and tools used to help enhance preparedness.

This lesson summarizes the information presented in Component I: Preparedness, including:

- Concepts and Principles
- Achieving Preparedness

Refer to pages 9 through 22 of the NIMS document.

Introduction to NIMS Preparedness

Image 3.3

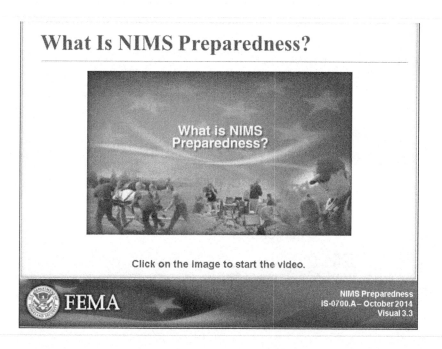

Key Points

This video provides an introduction to the NIMS Preparedness component.

Video Transcript: Given the threats we face; a lack of preparedness could have catastrophic consequences. Effective and coordinated emergency management and incident response require that we create a culture of preparedness.

National preparedness can only succeed through coordination at all levels of government and by forming strong partnerships with the private sector and nongovernmental organizations.

Preparation is a continuous cycle of planning, organizing, training, equipping, exercising, evaluating, and taking corrective action.

NIMS provides the mechanisms and tools to help enhance preparedness. Within NIMS, preparedness focuses on:

- Planning,
- Procedures and protocols,
- Training and exercises,
- Personnel qualification and certification, and
- Equipment certification.

The concepts and principles that form the basis for preparedness are the integration of the concepts and principles of all the components of NIMS.

This lesson introduces you to the NIMS Preparedness component.

Image 3.4

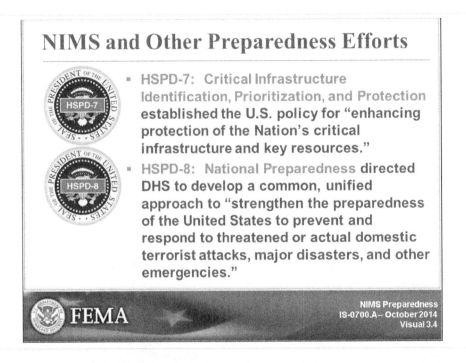

Key Points

Homeland Security Presidential Directive 5 (HSPD-5) established a single, comprehensive approach to incident management. Present the following key points about additional Homeland Security Presidential Directives linked to national preparedness:

- **HSPD-7: Critical Infrastructure Identification, Prioritization, and Protection** established the U.S. policy for "enhancing protection of the Nation's critical infrastructure and key resources" and mandates a national plan to implement that policy in partnership with Federal departments and agencies; State, tribal, and local governments; nongovernmental organizations; and the private sector.
- **HSPD-8: National Preparedness** directed DHS to lead a national initiative to develop a National Preparedness System—a common, unified approach to "strengthen the preparedness of the United States to prevent and respond to threatened or actual domestic terrorist attacks, major disasters, and other emergencies."

Image 3.5

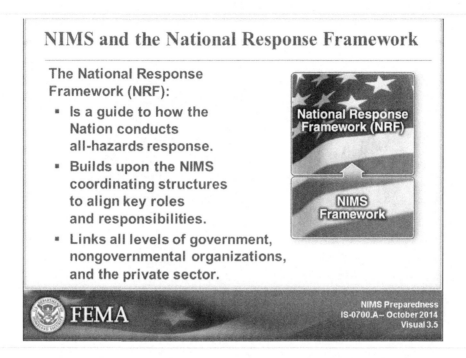

NIMS and the National Response Framework

The National Response Framework (NRF):

- Is a guide to how the Nation conducts all-hazards response.
- Builds upon the NIMS coordinating structures to align key roles and responsibilities.
- Links all levels of government, nongovernmental organizations, and the private sector.

National Response Framework (NRF)

NIMS Framework

FEMA

NIMS Preparedness
IS-0700.A – October 2014
Visual 3.5

Key Points

The National Response Framework (NRF):

- Is a guide to how the Nation conducts all-hazards response.
- Builds upon the NIMS coordinating structures to align key roles and responsibilities across the Nation, linking all levels of government, nongovernmental organizations, and the private sector.

A basic premise of both NIMS and the NRF is that incidents typically are managed at the local level first.

Following NIMS doctrine, the NRF is designed to ensure that local jurisdictions retain command, control, and authority over response activities for their jurisdictional areas.

Image 3.6

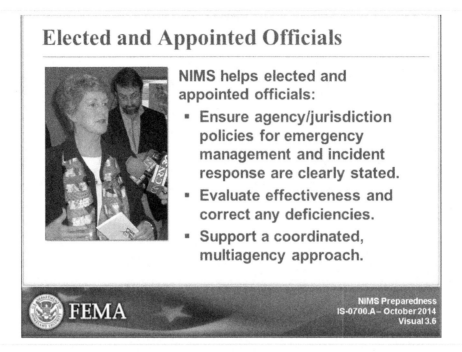

Key Points

To better serve their constituents, elected and appointed officials must understand and commit to NIMS.

NIMS provides elected and appointed officials with a framework to help:

- Ensure that agency/jurisdiction policies for emergency management and incident response are clearly stated.
- Evaluate effectiveness and correct any deficiencies.
- Support a coordinated, multiagency approach.

Although elected and appointed officials may not be at the scene of the incident, they should have the ability to communicate and support the on-scene command.

Image 3.7

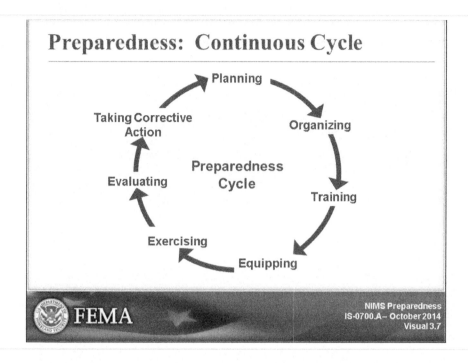

Key Points

Ongoing preparedness helps us to:

- Coordinate during times of crisis.
- Execute efficient and effective emergency management and incident response activities.

Preparedness is achieved and maintained through a continuous cycle of planning, organizing, training, equipping, exercising, evaluating, and taking corrective action.

Image 3.7

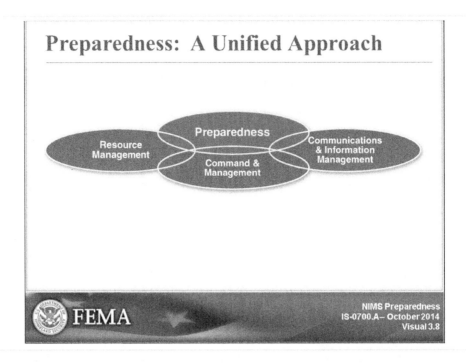

Key Points

Preparedness requires a unified approach to emergency management and incident response activities. To achieve a unified approach, components of NIMS should be integrated within the emergency management and incident response structure.

Preparedness should be integrated into resource management, command and management, and communications and information management to form an effective system.

Image 3.9

Levels of Capability

Inventorying and categorizing resources:

- Establishes and verifies the levels of capability needed.
- Identifies and verifies that resources possess the needed qualifications.

 FEMA

NIMS Preparedness
IS-0700.A – October 2014
Visual 3.9

Key Points

For NIMS to function effectively, jurisdictions and organizations should set expectations about the capabilities and resources that will be provided before, during, and after an incident.

Inventorying and categorizing of resources is a critical element of preparedness because it:

- Establishes and verifies the levels of capability needed based on risk and hazard assessments prior to an incident.
- Identifies and verifies that emergency response resources possess the needed qualifications during an incident.

Preparedness Mechanisms

Image 3.10

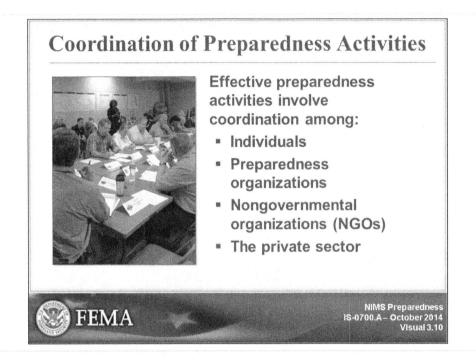

Key Points

Preparedness activities should be coordinated among all appropriate agencies and organizations within the jurisdiction, as well as across jurisdictions. Preparedness activities may involve the following groups:

- **Individuals:** Individuals should participate in their community's outreach programs that promote and support individual and community preparedness (e.g., public education, training sessions, demonstrations). These programs should include preparedness of those with special needs.
- **Preparedness Organizations:** Preparedness organizations provide coordination for emergency management and incident response activities before an incident or scheduled event. These organizations range from groups of individuals to small committees to large standing organizations that represent a wide variety of committees, planning groups, and other organizations (e.g., Citizen Corps, Local Emergency Planning Committees, Critical Infrastructure Sector Coordinating Councils).
- **Nongovernmental Organizations:** Nongovernmental organizations (NGOs), such as community-based, faith- based, or national organizations (e.g., the Salvation Army, National Voluntary Organizations Active in Disaster, and the American Red Cross), play vital support roles in emergency management and incident response activities. Compliance with NIMS is not mandated for NGOs. However, adherence to NIMS can help these organizations integrate into a jurisdiction's preparedness efforts. To ensure integration, capable and interested NGOs should be included in ongoing preparedness efforts, especially in planning, training, and exercises.
- **Private Sector:** The private sector plays a vital support role in emergency management and incident response and should be incorporated into all aspects of NIMS. Utilities, industries, corporations, businesses, and professional and trade associations typically are involved in critical aspects of emergency management and incident response. These organizations should prepare for all-hazards incidents that may affect their ability to deliver goods and services. It is essential that private-sector organizations that are directly involved in emergency management and incident response (e.g.,

hospitals, utilities, and critical infrastructure owners and operators) be included in a jurisdiction's preparedness efforts, as appropriate.

Governments at all levels should work with the private sector to establish a common set of expectations consistent with Federal, State, tribal, and local roles, responsibilities, and methods of operations. These expectations should be widely disseminated and the necessary training and practical exercises conducted so that they are thoroughly understood in advance of an actual incident.

Image 3.11

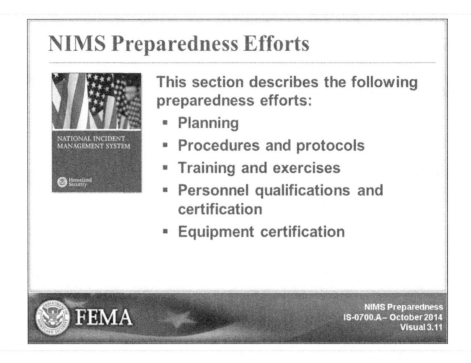

Key Points

Preparedness efforts should validate and maintain plans, policies, and procedures, describing how they will prioritize, coordinate, manage, and support information and resources. This section of the unit describes the following preparedness efforts:

- Planning
- Procedures and protocols
- Training and exercises
- Personnel qualifications and certification
- Equipment certification

Image 3.12

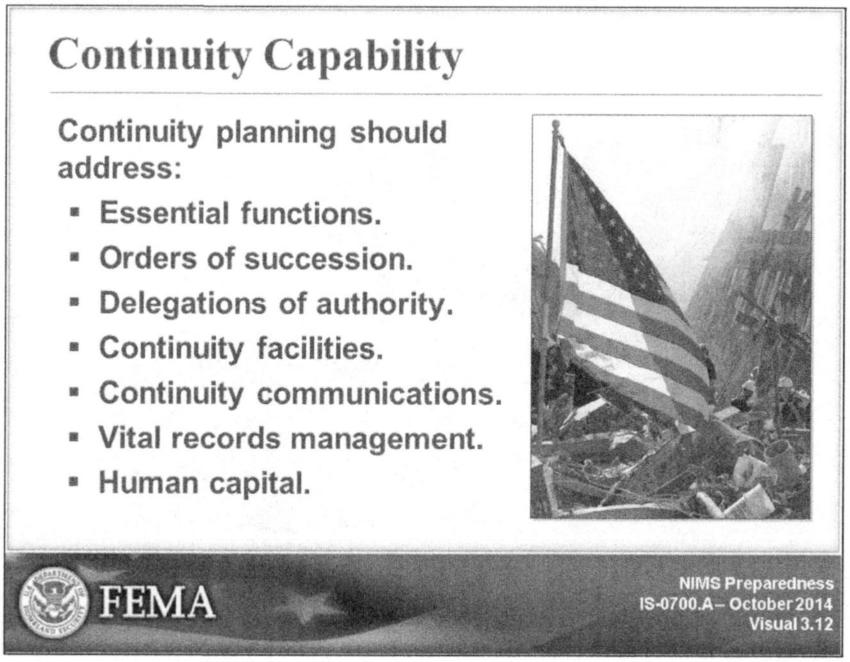

Continuity Capability

Continuity planning should address:

- Essential functions.
- Orders of succession.
- Delegations of authority.
- Continuity facilities.
- Continuity communications.
- Vital records management.
- Human capital.

FEMA

NIMS Preparedness
IS-0700.A – October 2014
Visual 3.12

Key Points

Recent natural and manmade disasters have demonstrated the need for building continuity capability as part of preparedness efforts.

Continuity planning should be instituted within all organizations (including all levels of government and the private sector) and address such things as:

- Essential functions.
- Orders of succession.
- Delegations of authority.
- Continuity facilities.
- Continuity communications.
- Vital records management.
- Human capital.

NSPD-51/HSPD-20 and Federal Continuity Directive 1, dated February 4, 2007, outline the continuity requirements for all Federal departments and agencies (with guidance for non-Federal organizations).

Image 3.13

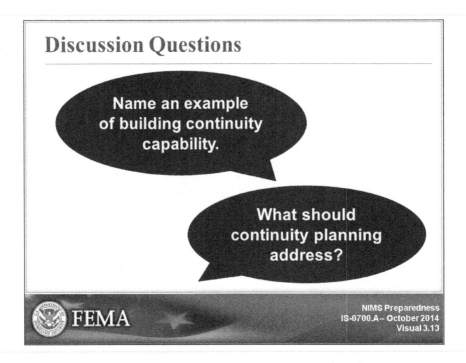

Key Points

Answer the following discussion questions:

- **Name an example of building continuity capability.**

- **What should continuity planning address?**

Image 3.14

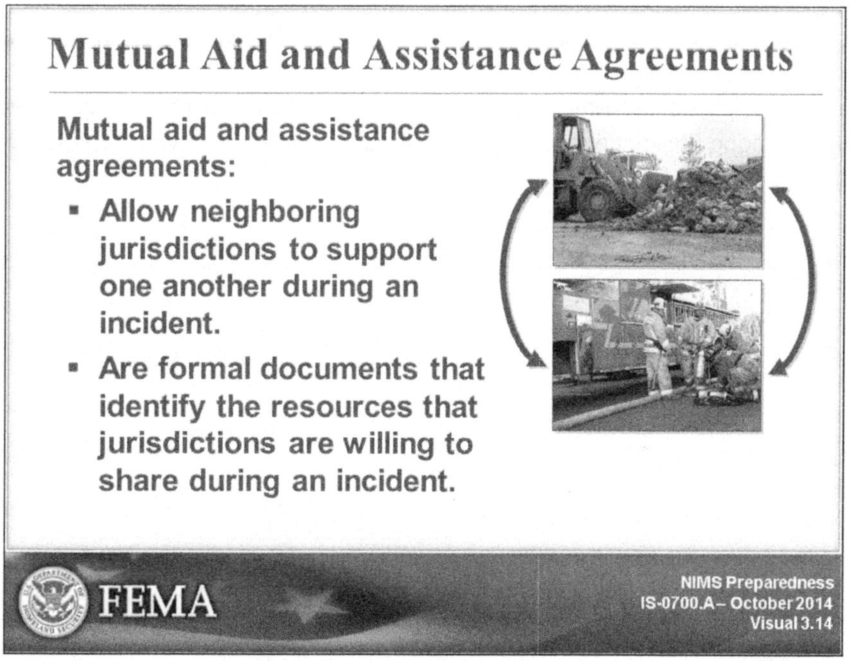

Mutual Aid and Assistance Agreements

Mutual aid and assistance agreements:

- Allow neighboring jurisdictions to support one another during an incident.
- Are formal documents that identify the resources that jurisdictions are willing to share during an incident.

FEMA

NIMS Preparedness
IS-0700.A – October 2014
Visual 3.14

Key Points

Mutual aid agreements and assistance agreements provide a mechanism to quickly obtain emergency assistance in the form of personnel, equipment, materials, and other associated services. Explain that NIMS encourages:

- Jurisdictions to enter into mutual aid and assistance agreements with other jurisdictions and/or organizations from which they expect to receive, or to which they expect to provide, assistance.
- States to participate in interstate compacts and to consider establishing intrastate agreements that encompass all local jurisdictions.

Agreements among all parties providing or requesting resources help to enable effective and efficient resource management during incident operations. Tell the participants that they might want to consider developing and maintaining standing agreements and contracts for services and supplies that may be needed during an incident.

There are several types of these kinds of agreements, including but not limited to the following:

- **Automatic Mutual Aid:** Agreements that permit the automatic dispatch and response of requested resources without incident-specific approvals. These agreements are usually basic contracts; some may be informal accords.
- **Local Mutual Aid:** Agreements between neighboring jurisdictions or organizations that involve a formal request for assistance and generally cover a larger geographic area than automatic mutual aid.
- **Regional Mutual Aid:** Substate regional mutual aid agreements between multiple jurisdictions that are often sponsored by a council of governments or a similar regional body.
- **Statewide/Intrastate Mutual Aid:** Agreements, often coordinated through the State, that incorporate both State and local governmental and nongovernmental assets in an attempt to increase preparedness statewide.
- **Interstate Agreements:** Out-of-State assistance through formal State-to-State agreements such as the

Emergency Management Assistance Compact, or other formal State-to-State agreements that support the response effort.

- **International Agreements:** Agreements between the United States and other nations for the exchange of Federal assets in an emergency.
- **Other Agreements:** Any agreement, whether formal or informal, used to request or provide assistance and/or resources among jurisdictions at any level of government (including foreign), NGOs, or the private sector.

Image 3.15

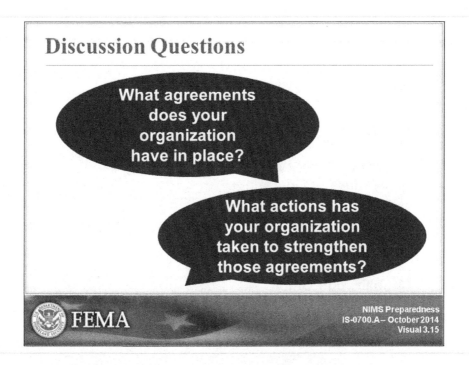

Key Points

Anser the following discussion questions:

- **What agreements does your organization have in place?**

- **What actions has your organization taken to strengthen those agreements?**

Preparedness Tools

Image 3.16

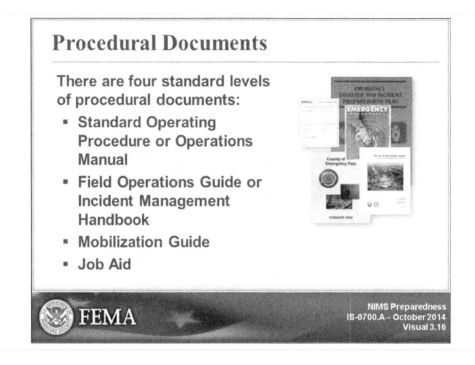

Key Points

Effective preparedness involves documenting specific procedures to follow before, during, and after an incident.

Procedural documents should detail the specific actions to implement a plan or system. There are four standard levels of procedural documents:

- **Standard Operating Procedure or Operations Manual:** Complete reference document that provides the purpose, authorities, duration, and details for the preferred method of performing a single function or a number of interrelated functions in a uniform manner.
- **Field Operations Guide or Incident Management Handbook:** Durable pocket or desk guide that contains essential information required to perform specific assignments or functions.
- **Mobilization Guide:** Reference document used by agencies/organizations outlining agreements, processes, and procedures used by all participating organizations for activating, assembling, and transporting resources.
- **Job Aid:** Checklist or other visual aid intended to ensure that specific steps for completing a task or assignment are accomplished. Job aids serve as training aids to teach individuals how to complete specific job tasks.

Image 3.17

Protocols

Protocols:

- **Are sets of established guidelines for actions under various specified conditions.**
- **Permit the rapid execution of a task, a function, or a number of interrelated functions without having to seek permission.**

 **FEMA**

NIMS Preparedness
IS-0700.A – October 2014
Visual 3.17

Key Points

Protocols are sets of established guidelines for actions (which may be designated by individuals, teams, functions, or capabilities) under various specified conditions.

Establishing protocols provides for the standing orders, authorizations, and delegations necessary to permit the rapid execution of a task, a function, or a number of interrelated functions without having to seek permission.

Protocols permit specific personnel—based on training and delegation of authority—to assess a situation, take immediate steps to intervene, and escalate their efforts to a specific level before further guidance or authorizations are required.

Image 3.18

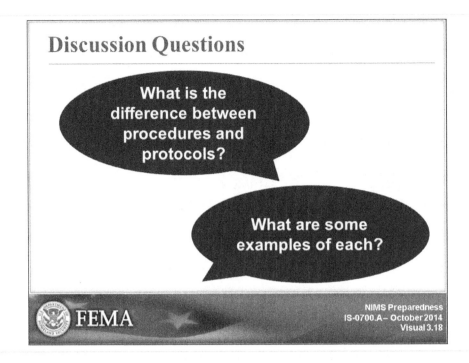

Key Points

Answer the following discussion questions:

- **What is the difference between procedures and protocols?**

- **What are some examples of each?**

Image 3.19

Training

Training should allow practitioners to:

- Use the concepts and principles of NIMS in exercises, planned events, and actual incidents.
- Become more comfortable using NIMS, including the Incident Command System.

FEMA

NIMS Preparedness
IS-0700.A – October 2014
Visual 3.19

Key Points

Personnel with roles in emergency management and incident response should be appropriately trained to improve all-hazards capabilities nationwide. Training should allow practitioners to:

- Use the concepts and principles of NIMS in exercises, planned events, and actual incidents.
- Become more comfortable using NIMS, including the Incident Command System.

Training and exercises should be specifically tailored to the responsibilities of the personnel involved in incident management. The National Integration Center (NIC) has developed requirements and guidance for NIMS training materials.

Image 3.20

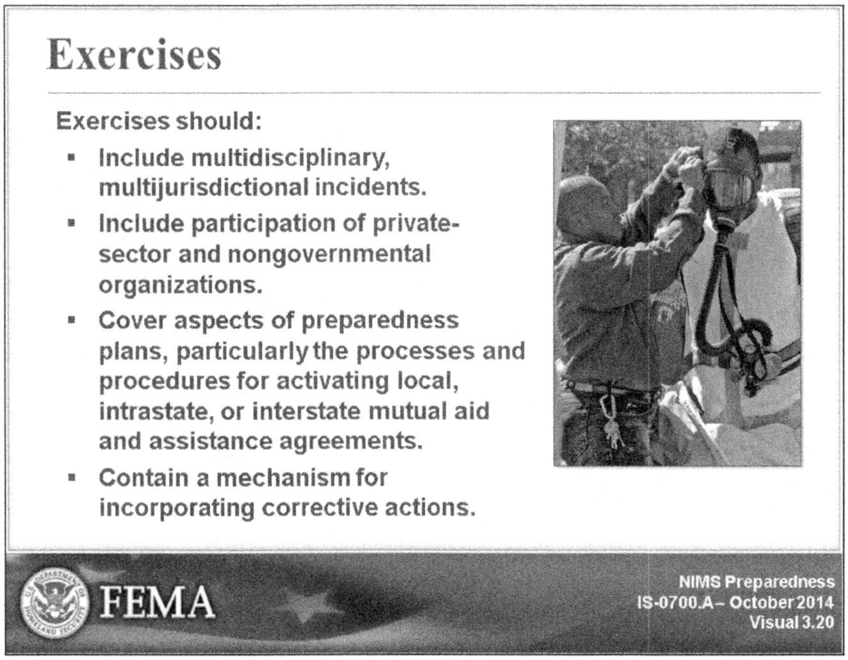

Exercises

Exercises should:

- Include multidisciplinary, multijurisdictional incidents.
- Include participation of private-sector and nongovernmental organizations.
- Cover aspects of preparedness plans, particularly the processes and procedures for activating local, intrastate, or interstate mutual aid and assistance agreements.
- Contain a mechanism for incorporating corrective actions.

FEMA

NIMS Preparedness
IS-0700.A– October 2014
Visual 3.20

Key Points

To improve NIMS performance, emergency management/response personnel need to participate in realistic exercises. Exercises should:

- Include multidisciplinary, multijurisdictional incidents.
- Require interactions with the private sector and nongovernmental organizations.
- Cover all aspects of preparedness plans, particularly the processes and procedures for activating local, intrastate, and/or interstate mutual aid agreements and assistance agreements.
- Contain a mechanism for incorporating corrective actions and lessons learned from incidents into the planning process.

Image 3.21

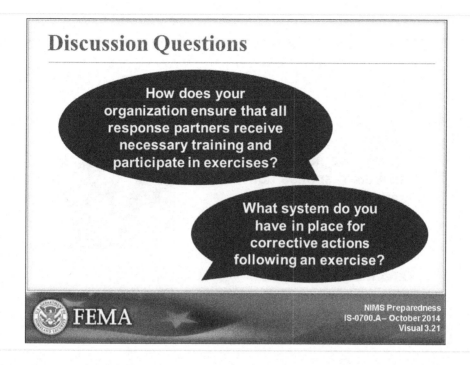

Key Points

Answer the following discussion questions:

- **How does your organization ensure that all response partners receive necessary training and participate in exercises?**

- **What system do you have in place for corrective actions following an exercise?**

Image 3.22

Personnel Qualifications and Certification

Standards:

- Help ensure that personnel possess the minimum knowledge, skills, and experience necessary to execute response activities safely and effectively.
- Typically include training, experience, credentialing, validation, and physical and medical fitness.

NIMS Preparedness
IS-0700.A – October 2014
Visual 3.22

Key Points

A critical element of NIMS preparedness is the use of national standards that allow for common or compatible structures for the qualification, licensure, and certification of emergency management/response personnel. Standards:

- Help ensure that personnel possess the minimum knowledge, skills, and experience necessary to execute incident management and emergency response activities safely and effectively.
- Typically include training, experience, credentialing, validation, and physical and medical fitness.

The baseline criteria for voluntary credentialing will be established by the National Integration Center.

Image 3.23

Equipment Certification

Equipment certification:

- Helps ensure that the equipment acquired will perform to certain standards.
- Supports planning and rapid fulfillment of needs based on a common understanding of the abilities of distinct types of equipment.

NIMS Preparedness
IS-0700.A– October 2014
Visual 3.23

Key Points

We all count on having the right tools to do the job. Being able to certify equipment is a critical component of preparedness. Explain that equipment certification:

- Helps ensure that the equipment acquired will perform to certain standards (as designated by organizations such as the National Fire Protection Association or National Institute of Standards and Technology).
- Supports planning and rapid fulfillment of needs based on a common understanding of the abilities of distinct types of equipment.

Image 3.24

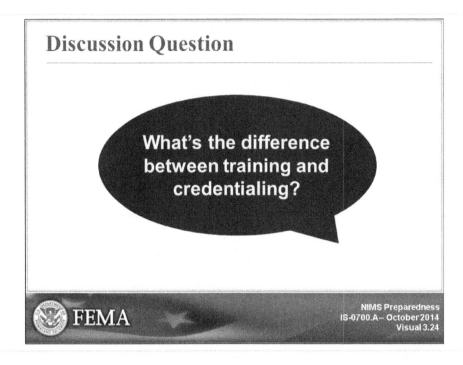

Key Points

Answer the following discussion question:

- **What is the difference between training and credentialing?**

Image 3.25

Mitigation and Preparedness

Mitigation:

- **Reduces the loss of life and property.**
- **Minimizes damage to the environment from natural or manmade disasters.**
- **Helps avoid or lessen the impact of a disaster.**
- **Impedes the cycle of disaster damage, reconstruction, and repeated damage.**

 **FEMA**

NIMS Preparedness
IS-0700.A– October 2014
Visual 3.25

Key Points

Mitigation is an important element of emergency management and incident response. Mitigation:

- Provides a critical foundation in the effort to reduce the loss of life and property and to minimize damage to the environment from natural or manmade disasters by avoiding or lessening the impact of a disaster.
- Provides value to the public by creating safer communities and impeding the cycle of disaster damage, reconstruction, and repeated damage. These activities or actions, in most cases, will have a long-term sustained effect.

Preparedness planning and mitigation planning are complementary processes that should support one another. Examples of mitigation activities include the following:

- Ongoing public education and outreach activities designed to reduce loss of life and destruction of property.
- Complying with or exceeding floodplain management and land-use regulations.
- Enforcing stringent building codes, seismic design standards, and wind-bracing requirements for new construction, or repairing or retrofitting existing buildings.
- Supporting measures to ensure the protection and resilience of critical infrastructure and key resources designed to ensure business continuity and the economic stability of
- communities.
- Acquiring damaged homes or businesses in flood-prone areas, relocating the structures, and returning the property to open space, wetlands, or recreational uses.
- Identifying, utilizing, and refurbishing shelters and safe rooms to help protect people in their homes, public buildings, and schools in hurricane- and tornado-prone areas.
- Implementing a vital records program at all levels of government to prevent loss of crucial documents and records.
- Intelligence sharing and linkage leading to other law enforcement activities, such as infiltration of a terrorist cell to prevent an attack.

- Periodic remapping of hazard or potential hazard zones, using geospatial techniques.
- Management of data regarding historical incidents to support strategic planning and analysis.
- Development of hazard-specific evacuation routes.

Knowledge Review and Summary

Image 3.26

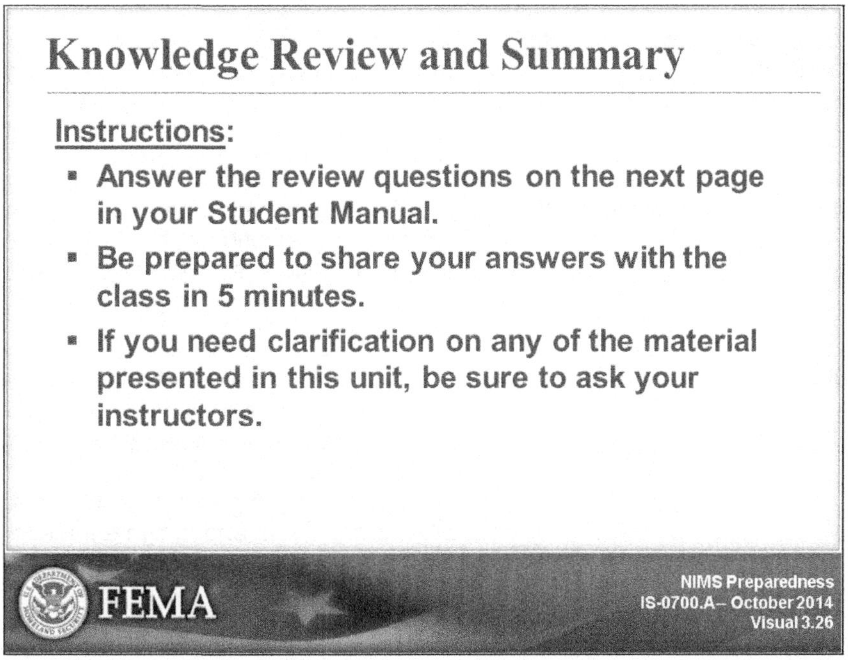

Knowledge Review and Summary

Instructions:

- Answer the review questions on the next page in your Student Manual.
- Be prepared to share your answers with the class in 5 minutes.
- If you need clarification on any of the material presented in this unit, be sure to ask your instructors.

 FEMA

NIMS Preparedness
IS-0700.A– October 2014
Visual 3.26

Key Points

Instructions:

- Answer the review questions on the next page.
- Be prepared to share your answers with the class in 5 minutes.
- If you need clarification on any of the material presented in this unit, ask your instructors.

Unit 3: Knowledge Review

1. Match the document on the left by writing in the letter with the correct matching statement on the right.

Document Title	Description
_____ Homeland Security Presidential Directive 5 (HSPD-5)	A. Provides the structure and mechanisms to ensure effective Federal support of State, tribal, and local related activities.
_____ National Response Framework (NRF)	B. Requires all Federal departments and agencies to make adoption of NIMS by State, tribal, and local organizations a condition for Federal preparedness assistance (through grants, contracts, and other activities).
_____ National Incident Management System (NIMS)	C. Describes a set of principles that provides a systematic, proactive approach guiding government agencies at all levels, nongovernmental organizations, and the private sector to work seamlessly to prevent, protect against, respond to, recover from, and mitigate the effects of incidents.

2. What is a basic premise of the NIMS and the NRF?

3. What is one action that elected and appointed officials do to better serve their constituents?

4. Review the actions below. Indicate if the action is consistent with NIMS preparedness principles.

	Consistent with NIMS	Not Consistent with NIMS
A jurisdiction is inventorying and categorizing resources (e.g, personnel, equipment, supplies, and facilities) to establish and verify levels of capability prior to an incident.	☐	☐
To expedite NIMS compliance, a team has been tasked to complete a preparedness plan while other teams independently address the other NIMS components.	☐	☐
An agency has established a mechanism for incorporating corrective actions into the planning process following the evaluation of an exercise.	☐	☐
Elected officials are participating in a multijurisdictional exercise not on scene but rather in a unified policy role at a joint operations center.	☐	☐

5.   What mechanism's primary objective is to facilitate rapid, short-term deployment of emergency support prior to, during, and/or after an incident?

6.   Use the space below to make note of any questions you have about the material covered in this unit.

Preparedness Self-Assessment

Image 3.27

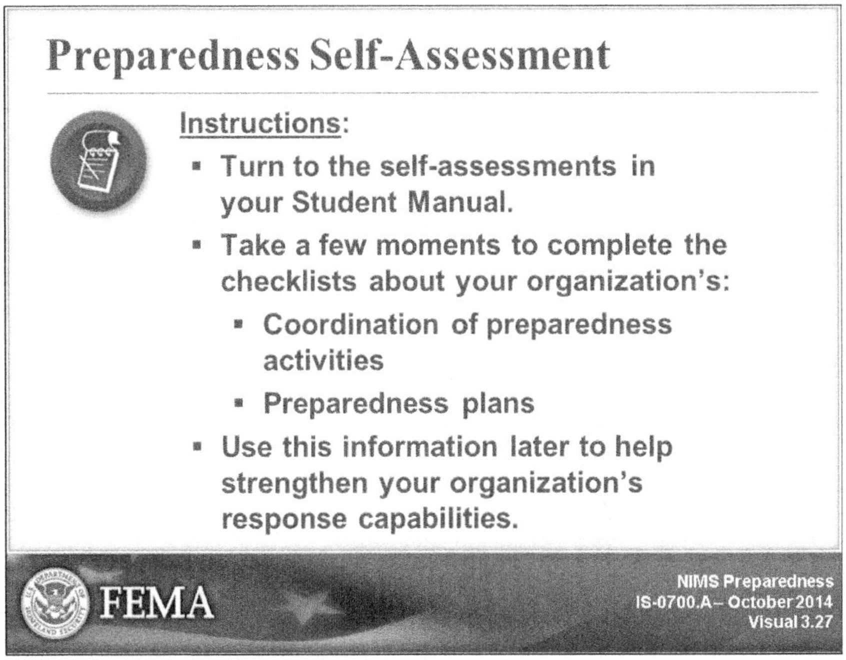

Preparedness Self-Assessment

<u>Instructions</u>:
- **Turn to the self-assessments in your Student Manual.**
- **Take a few moments to complete the checklists about your organization's:**
  - **Coordination of preparedness activities**
  - **Preparedness plans**
- **Use this information later to help strengthen your organization's response capabilities.**

NIMS Preparedness
IS-0700.A– October 2014
Visual 3.27

Key Points

Instructions:

- Turn to the self-assessments in your Student Manual.
- Take a few moments to complete the checklists about your organization's:
  - Coordination of preparedness activities
  - Preparedness plans
- Use this information later to help strengthen your organization's response capabilities.

Self-Assessment: Coordination of Preparedness Activities

Purpose: Preparedness activities should be coordinated among all appropriate agencies and organizations within the jurisdiction, as well as across jurisdictions.

Instructions: Complete the following self-assessment to assess your jurisdiction's, agency's, or organization's coordination of preparedness activities. Use this information to ensure that your jurisdiction, agency, or organization is coordinating its preparedness efforts with all appropriate parties, including:

- Individuals
- Preparedness Organizations
- Nongovernmental Organizations
- Private Sector

Preparedness Activities	Yes	No	N/A
Appropriate outreach programs are used to promote and support individual and community preparedness (e.g., public education, training sessions, demonstrations), including preparedness of those with special needs.	☐	☐	☐
Preparedness organizations (e.g., Citizen Corps, Community Emergency Response Teams, Local Emergency Planning Committees, Critical Infrastructure Sector Coordinating Councils) are included in planning prior to an incident or planned event.	☐	☐	☐
Interested and capable nongovernmental organizations, such as community-based, faith-based, or national voluntary organizations, are included in ongoing preparedness efforts, especially in planning, training, and exercises.	☐	☐	☐
Partnerships are formed with the private sector (e.g., utilities, industries, corporations, businesses, and professional and trade associations) to prepare for all-hazards incidents that may affect their ability to deliver goods and services.	☐	☐	☐

Are there any additional groups that should be included in these preparation efforts? Use the space below to make note of action items for your jurisdiction, agency, or organization.

Self-Assessment: Preparedness Plans

Purpose: Effective and coordinated incident response requires that we embrace a preparedness ethic. The concepts and principles that form the basis for preparedness are the integration of the concepts and principles of all the components of NIMS.

Instructions: Complete the following self-assessment to assess your jurisdiction's, agency's, or organization's coordination of preparedness activities. Use this information to ensure that your jurisdiction, agency, or organization is coordinating its preparedness activities effectively.

Preparedness Plans	Yes	No
Are based on hazard identification and risk analysis.	☐	☐
Define organizational structures, roles and responsibilities, policies, and protocols for providing support.	☐	☐
Describe how personnel, equipment, and other governmental and nongovernmental resources will be used to support emergency management and incident response requirements.	☐	☐

Incorporate advance planning associated with responder protection, resource management, and communications and information management. Incorporate strategies for maintaining continuity of government and continuity of operations during and after incidents.	☐	☐
Provide mechanisms to ensure resiliency of critical infrastructure and economic stability of communities. Incorporate a clearly defined process for seeking and requesting assistance including procedures for activating mutual aid agreements and assistance agreements.	☐	☐
Are coordinated and complement one another (i.e., response, mitigation, and recovery plans). Form the basis of training and credentialing personnel.	☐	☐
Are exercised periodically to ensure that all individuals involved in response are able to execute their assigned tasks.	☐	☐
Include public awareness, education, and communications plans and protocols.	☐	☐
Are updated periodically to reflect changes in the emergency management and incident response environment, as well as any institutional or organizational changes.	☐	☐

Use the space below to make note of action items for your jurisdiction, agency, or organization.

66

UNIT 4: NIMS COMMUNICATIONS AND INFORMATION MANAGEMENT

Objectives

At the end of this unit, you should be able to:

- Describe the importance of communications and information management.
- Define the concepts of common operating picture and interoperability.
- Describe the purpose of communications and information management standards, procedures, and protocols.

Scope

- Unit Introduction and Objectives
  - Video: What is NIMS Communications and Information Management?
- Characteristics of Effective Communications Systems
  - Flexible Communications and Information Systems
  - Common Operating Picture
  - Interoperability
  - Reliability, Portability, Scalability
  - Resiliency and Redundancy
  - Activity
- Standards, Procedures, and Protocols
  - Standardized Communications Types
  - Policy and Planning
  - Agreements
  - Equipment Standards and Training
  - Incident Information
  - Communications and Data Standards
  - Plain Language & Common Terminology
- Knowledge Review and Summary
- Preparedness Self-Assessment

Unit Introduction and Objectives

Image 4.1

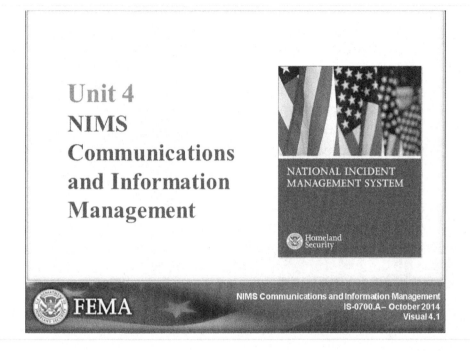

Key Points

This unit presents an overview of the NIMS Communications and Information Management component.

Image 4.2

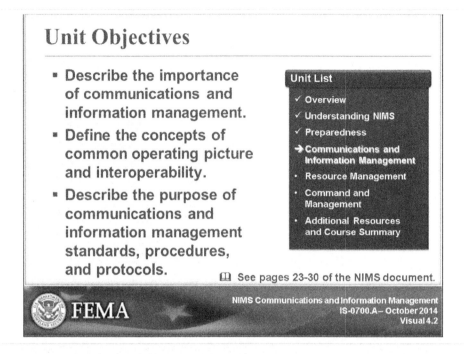

Key Points

At the end of this unit, you should be able to:

- Describe the importance of communications and information management.
- Define the concepts of common operating picture and interoperability.
- Describe the purpose of communications and information management standards, procedures, and protocols.

This unit summarizes the information presented in Component II: Communications and Information Management, including:

- Concepts and Principles
- Management Characteristics
- Organization and Operations

Refer to pages 23 through 30 of the NIMS document.

Video

Image 4.3

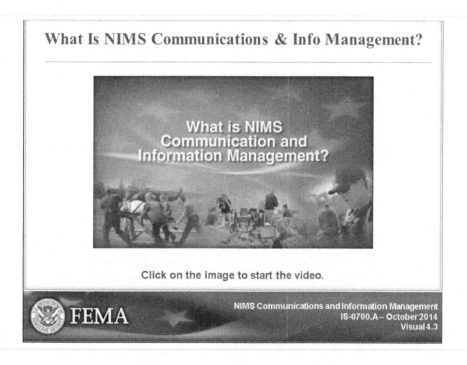

Key Points

This video provides an introduction to the NIMS Communications and Information Management component.

Video Transcript: Effective emergency response depends on communication—the ability to maintain a common operating picture through the constant flow of information.

During and after Hurricane Katrina, communications systems failed, severely hampering information flow and response operations. In New Orleans, most of the city was flooded. The combined effects of wind, rain, storm surge, breached levees, and flooding knocked out virtually the entire infrastructure—electrical power, roads, water supply and sewage, and communications systems.

Thomas Stone, Fire Chief, St. Bernard Parish: "We lost our communications system, and when you are not able to communicate, you can't coordinate your response. You never think that you will lose your entire infrastructure."

Communications problems are not limited to systems being destroyed or not functioning. Similar problems arise when agencies cannot exchange needed information because of incompatible systems. NIMS identifies several important features of public safety communications and information systems.

Communications systems need to be:

- **Interoperable** – able to communicate within and across agencies and jurisdictions.
- **Reliable** – able to function in the context of any kind of emergency.
- **Portable** – built on standardized radio technologies, protocols, and frequencies.
- **Scalable** – suitable for use on a small or large scale as the needs of the incident dictate.
- **Resilient** – able to perform despite damaged or lost infrastructure.
- **Redundant** – able to use alternate communications methods when primary systems go out.

Regardless of the communications hardware being used, standardized procedures, protocols, and formats are necessary to gather, collate, synthesize, and disseminate incident information. And in a crisis, life-and-death decisions depend on the information we receive.

This lesson introduces you to the NIMS Communications and Information Management component.

Characteristics of Effective Communications Systems

Image 4.4

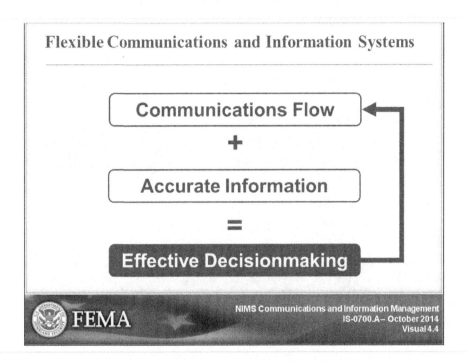

Key Points

All too often, after-action reports cite communications failures as an impediment to effective incident management.

Communications breakdowns are not limited to equipment and systems-related failures. The use of different protocols, codes instead of plain language, and non-standardized reporting formats hampers our ability to share critical information and make effective decisions.

To overcome these past problems, the NIMS Communications and Information Management component promotes the use of flexible communications and information systems.

Image 4.5

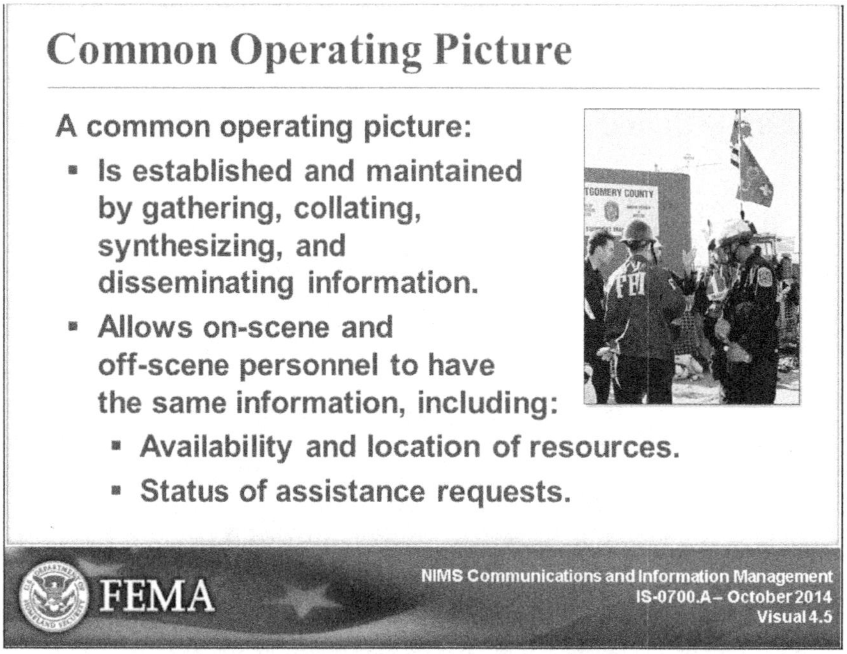

Key Points

A common operating picture is established and maintained by gathering, collating, synthesizing, and disseminating incident information to all appropriate parties.

Achieving a common operating picture allows on-scene and off- scene personnel—such as those at the Incident Command Post, Emergency Operations Center, or within a Multiagency Coordination Group—to have the same information about the incident, including the availability and location of resources and the status of assistance requests.

Image 4.6

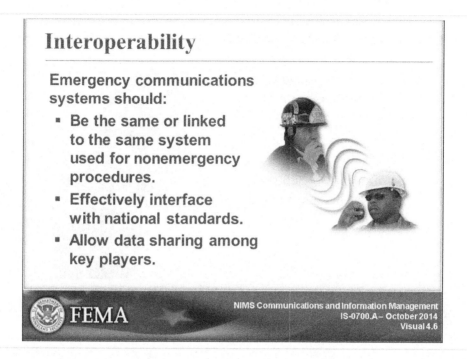

Key Points

First and foremost, **interoperability is the ability of emergency management/response personnel to interact and work well together.**

Interoperability also means that technical emergency communications systems should:

- Be the same or linked to the same system that the jurisdiction uses for nonemergency procedures.
- Effectively interface with national standards, as they are developed.
- Allow the sharing of data throughout the incident management process and among all key players.

Image 4.7

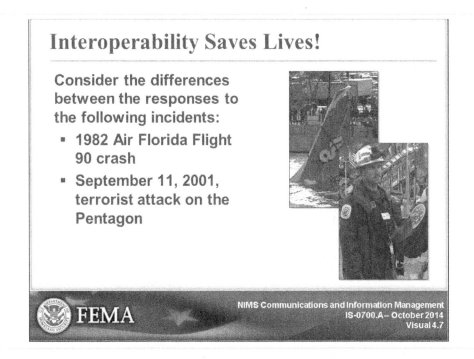

Key Points

The following examples to explain the value of interoperability:

Jan. 13, 1982: Air Florida Flight 90 crashed into the 14th St. Bridge in Washington, DC, during a snowstorm. More than 70 people lost their lives. Police, fire, and EMS crews responded quickly to the scene but experienced coordination problems because they could not communicate with one another.

Sept. 11, 2001: When American Airlines Flight 77 crashed into the Pentagon, 900 responders from 50 different agencies were able to communicate with one another. Response agencies had learned an invaluable lesson from the Air Florida tragedy. Regional coordination within the Washington area led to the adoption of the Incident Command System, establishment of interoperable communications protocols, and execution of mutual aid plans. The next challenge to solve was the lack of direct interoperability with secondary response agencies.

Image 4.8

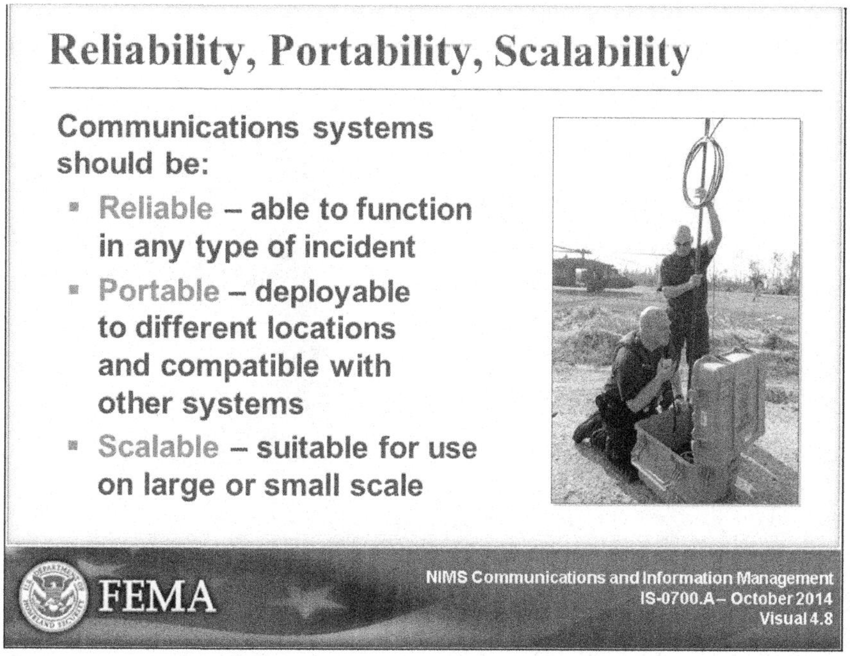

Key Points

To achieve interoperability, communications and information systems should be designed to be:

- **Reliable**—able to function in any type of incident, regardless of cause, size, location, or complexity.
- **Portable**—built on standardized radio technologies, protocols, and frequencies that allow communications systems to be deployed to different locations and integrated seamlessly with other systems.
- **Scalable**—suitable for use on a small or large scale, allowing for an increasing number of users.

Image 4.9

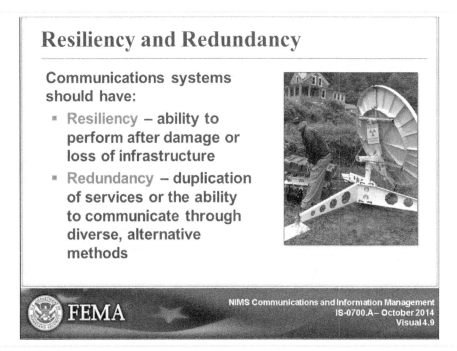

Key Points

Communications systems ensure that the flow of information will not be interrupted during an incident through:

- **Resiliency**—able to withstand and continue to perform after damage or loss of infrastructure.
- **Redundancy**—providing for either duplication of identical services or the ability to communicate through diverse, alternative methods when standard capabilities suffer damage.

Image 4.10

Activity

Instructions:
1. Work with your group to answer the questions below.
2. Select a spokesperson and be prepared in 5 minutes.

Questions:
- What steps have you taken to ensure a common operating picture among response partners?
- What interoperability challenges have you faced and how have you addressed them?
- How do you ensure that communications systems are reliable, scalable, and portable?
- What are some best practices for ensuring communications systems are resilient and redundant?

FEMA

NIMS Communications and Information Management
IS-0700.A – October 2014
Visual 4.10

Key Points

Instructions:

1. Work with your group to answer the questions below.
2. Select a spokesperson and be prepared in 5 minutes.

Questions:

- What steps have you taken to ensure a common operating picture among response partners?

- What interoperability challenges have you faced and how have you addressed them?

- How do you ensure that communications systems are reliable, scalable, and portable?

- What are some best practices for ensuring communications systems are resilient and redundant?

Standards, Procedures, and Protocols

Image 4.11

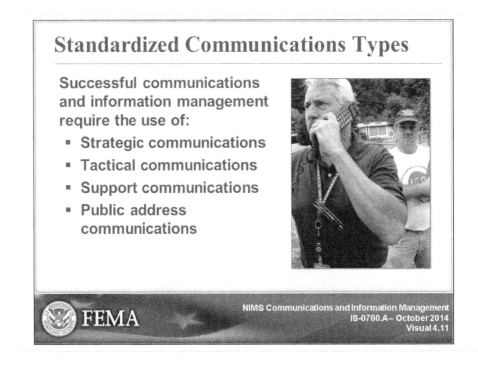

Key Points

Successful communications and information management require that emergency management/response personnel and their affiliated organizations use the following types of standardized communications:

- **Strategic Communications:** High-level directions, including resource priority decisions, roles and responsibilities determinations, and overall incident response courses of action.
- **Tactical Communications:** Communications between command and support elements and, as appropriate, cooperating agencies and organizations.
- **Support Communications:** Coordination in support of strategic and tactical communications (for example, communications among hospitals concerning resource ordering, dispatching, and tracking from logistics centers; traffic and public works communications).
- **Public Address Communications:** Emergency alerts and warnings, press conferences, etc.

The determination of the individual or agency/organization responsible for these communications is discussed in the NIMS Command and Management unit.

Image 4.12

> # Policy and Planning
>
> Communications plans should identify:
> - What information is essential and can be shared.
> - Who . . .
>   - Needs the information.
>   - Has the information.
> - How . . .
>   - Information will flow.
>   - Information is coordinated for public and media release.
>   - Communications systems will be used.
>
> **FEMA**　　　　NIMS Communications and Information Management
> IS-0700.A – October 2014
> Visual 4.12

Key Points

Coordinated communications policy and planning provide the basis for effective communications and information management.

All relevant stakeholders should be involved in planning sessions in order to formulate integrated communications plans and strategies. Technology and equipment standards also should be shared when appropriate, to provide stakeholders with the opportunity to be interoperable and compatible.

Sound communications management policies and plans should include information about the following aspects of communications and information management:

- Information needs should be defined by the jurisdiction/organization. These needs are often met at the Federal, State, tribal, and local levels, in concert with NGOs and the private sector, and primarily through preparedness organizations.
- The jurisdiction's or organization's information management system should provide guidance, standards, and tools to enable the integration of information needs into a common operating picture when needed.
- Procedures and protocols for the release of warnings, incident notifications, public communications, and other critical information are disseminated through a defined combination of networks used by the Emergency Operations Center. Notifications are made to the appropriate jurisdictional levels and to NGOs and the private sector through defined mechanisms specified in emergency operations and incident action plans.
- Agencies at all levels should plan in advance for the effective and efficient use of information management technologies (e.g., computers, networks, and information-sharing mechanisms) to integrate all command, coordination, and support functions involved in incident management and to enable the sharing of critical information and the cataloging of required corrective actions.

Image 4.13

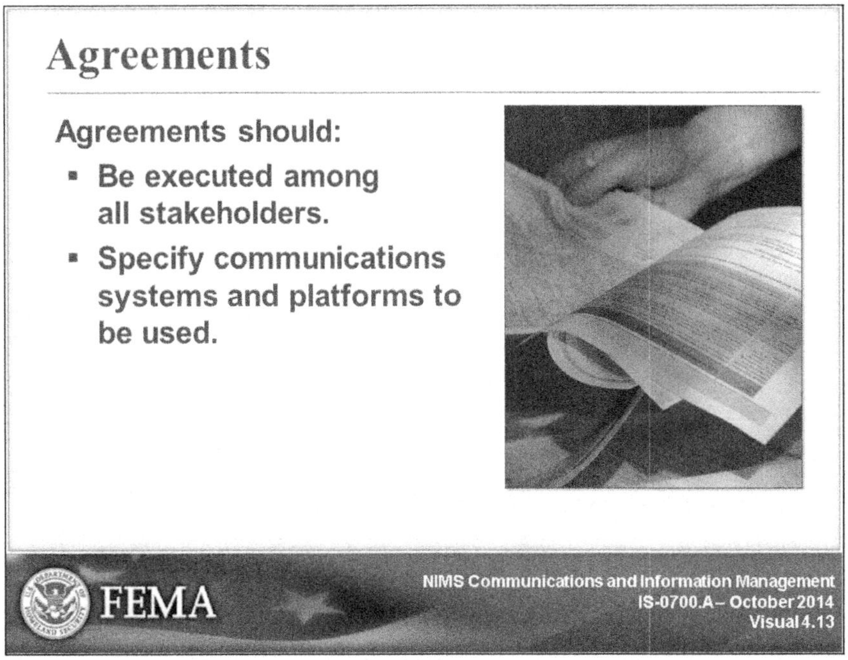

Agreements

Agreements should:

- Be executed among all stakeholders.
- Specify communications systems and platforms to be used.

FEMA

NIMS Communications and Information Management
IS-0700.A – October 2014
Visual 4.13

Key Points

Agreements should be executed among all stakeholders to ensure that the elements within plans and procedures will be in effect at the time of an incident.

Agreements should specify all of the communications systems and platforms through which the parties agree to use or share information.

Image 4.14

Equipment Standards and Training

Standards should address:

- **Conditions under which communications systems must operate**

- **Maintenance and updating of systems and equipment**

- **Periodic testing of systems**

FEMA

NIMS Communications and Information Management
IS-0700.A – October 2014
Visual 4.14

Key Points

Standards help ensure a seamless interface between communications systems, especially between the public and private sectors. Standards should address:

- The wide range of conditions under which communications systems must operate.
- The need for maintenance and updating of the systems and equipment.
- The periodic testing of systems.

Periodic training and exercises are essential so that personnel capabilities and limitations of communications plans and systems are addressed before an incident.

Image 4.15

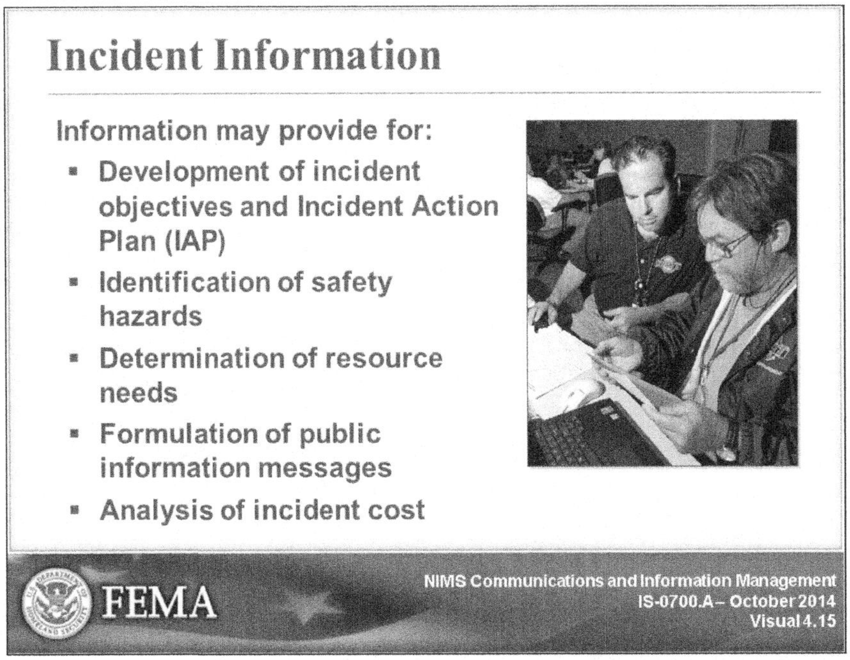

Incident Information

Information may provide for:

- Development of incident objectives and Incident Action Plan (IAP)
- Identification of safety hazards
- Determination of resource needs
- Formulation of public information messages
- Analysis of incident cost

FEMA

NIMS Communications and Information Management
IS-0700.A – October 2014
Visual 4.15

Key Points

Shared information is vital to the Incident Commander, Unified Command, and decisionmakers within supporting agencies and organizations. A single piece of information may provide input for development of incident objectives and the Incident Action Plan (IAP), identification of safety hazards, determination of resource needs, formulation of public information messages, and analysis of incident cost.

The following examples of information generated by an incident that can be used for decisionmaking purposes:

- **Incident Notification, Situation, and Status Reports**: Incident reporting and documentation procedures should be standardized to ensure that situational awareness is maintained and that emergency management/response personnel have easy access to critical information. Situation reports offer a snapshot of the past operational period and contain confirmed or verified information regarding the explicit details (who, what, when, where, and how) relating to the incident. Status reports, which may be contained in situation reports, relay information specifically related to the status of resources (e.g., availability or assignment of resources).
- **Analytical Data:** Data, such as information on public health and environmental monitoring, should be collected in a manner that observes standard data collection techniques and definitions. The data should then be transmitted using standardized analysis processes. During incidents that require public health and environmental sampling, multiple organizations at different levels of government often collect data, so standardization of data collection and analysis is critical. Additionally, standardization of sampling and data collection enables more reliable analysis and improves the quality of assessments provided to decisionmakers.
- **Geospatial Information:** Geospatial information is defined as information pertaining to the geographic location and characteristics of natural or constructed features and boundaries. It is often used to integrate assessments, situation reports, and incident notification into a common operating picture and as a data fusion and analysis tool to synthesize many kinds and sources of data and imagery. The use of geospatial data (and the recognition of its intelligence capabilities) is increasingly important during incidents. Geospatial information capabilities (such as nationally consistent grid systems or global

positioning systems based on lines of longitude and latitude) should be managed through preparedness efforts and integrated within the command, coordination, and support elements of an incident, including resource management and public information.

Image 4.16

Communications and Data Standards

Standards may include:

- A standard set of organizational structures and responsibilities.
- Common "typing" of communications resources.
- Use of agreed-upon communications protocols.
- Common identifier "titles" for personnel, facilities, and operational locations.

FEMA

NIMS Communications and Information Management
IS-0700.A – October 2014
Visual 4.16

Key Points

Communications and data standards are established to allow diverse organizations to work together effectively. Standards may include:

- A standard set of organizational structures and responsibilities.
- Common "typing" of communications resources to reflect specific capabilities.
- Use of agreed-upon communications protocols.
- Common identifier "titles" for personnel, facilities, and operational locations used to support incident operations.

Image 4.17

Plain Language & Common Terminology

Plain language:

- **Is a matter of safety.**
- **Facilitates interoperability across agencies/ organizations, jurisdictions, and disciplines.**
- **Ensures that information dissemination is timely, clear, acknowledged, and understood by all intended recipients.**

 **FEMA**

NIMS Communications and Information Management
IS-0700.A – October 2014
Visual 4.17

Key Points

The use of plain language in emergency management and incident response:

- Is a matter of safety.
- Facilitates interoperability across agencies/organizations, jurisdictions, and disciplines.
- Ensures that information dissemination is timely, clear, acknowledged, and understood by all intended recipients.

Codes should not be used, and all communications should be confined to essential messages. The use of acronyms should be avoided during incidents requiring the participation of multiple agencies or organizations.

When necessary, information may need to be encrypted so that security can be maintained

Although plain language may be appropriate during response to most incidents, tactical language is occasionally warranted due to the nature of the incident (e.g., during an ongoing terrorist event).

The protocols for using specialized encryption and tactical language should be incorporated into the Incident Action Plan or incident management communications plan.

Image 4.18

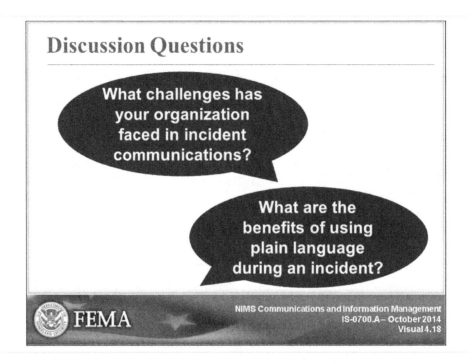

Key Points

Answer the following discussion questions:

- **What challenges has your organization faced in incident communications? How were they addressed?**

- **What are the benefits of using plain language and common terminology during an incident?**

Knowledge Review and Summary

Image 4.19

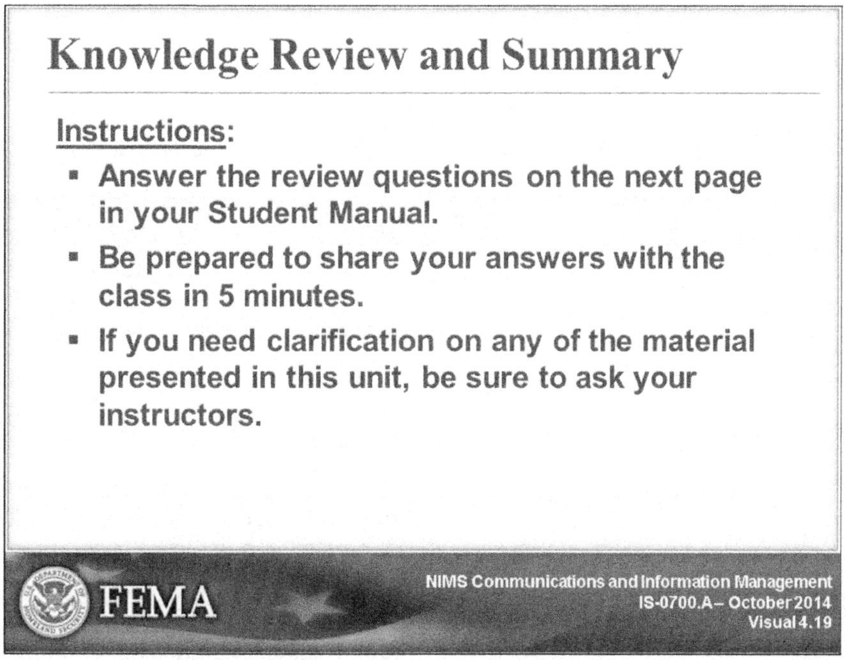

Knowledge Review and Summary

Instructions:

- Answer the review questions on the next page in your Student Manual.
- Be prepared to share your answers with the class in 5 minutes.
- If you need clarification on any of the material presented in this unit, be sure to ask your instructors.

 FEMA

NIMS Communications and Information Management
IS-0700.A – October 2014
Visual 4.19

Key Points

Instructions:

- Answer the review questions on the next page.
- Be prepared to share your answers with the class in 5 minutes.
- If you need clarification on any of the material presented in this unit, ask your instructors.

Unit 4: Knowledge Review

1. What is "an overview of an incident by all relevant parties that provides incident information enabling the Incident Commander/Unified Command and any supporting agencies and organizations to make effective, consistent, and timely decisions"?

2. Match the term on the left by writing in the letter with the correct matching definition on the right.

Term	Description
_____ Reliability	A. Communication systems have been designed with sufficient expandable capacity for routine responses as well as more major incidents.
_____ Portability	B. Physical protections have been installed to secure a computer network and communications equipment.
_____ Scalability	C. Exercises are conducted to test that systems are able to function in any type of incident, regardless of cause, size, location, or complexity.
_____ Resiliency	D. Backup power systems have been installed to maintain communications systems. Alternate communications devices, such as satellite phones, are available if standard capabilities suffer damage.
_____ Redundancy	E. All equipment acquired complies with standardized radio technologies, protocols, and frequencies to ensure that it will operate at different locations and integrate seamless with other systems.

3. What is interoperability? Why is it Important?

4. Use the space below to make note of any questions you have about the material covered in this unit.

Preparedness Self-Assessment

Image 4.20

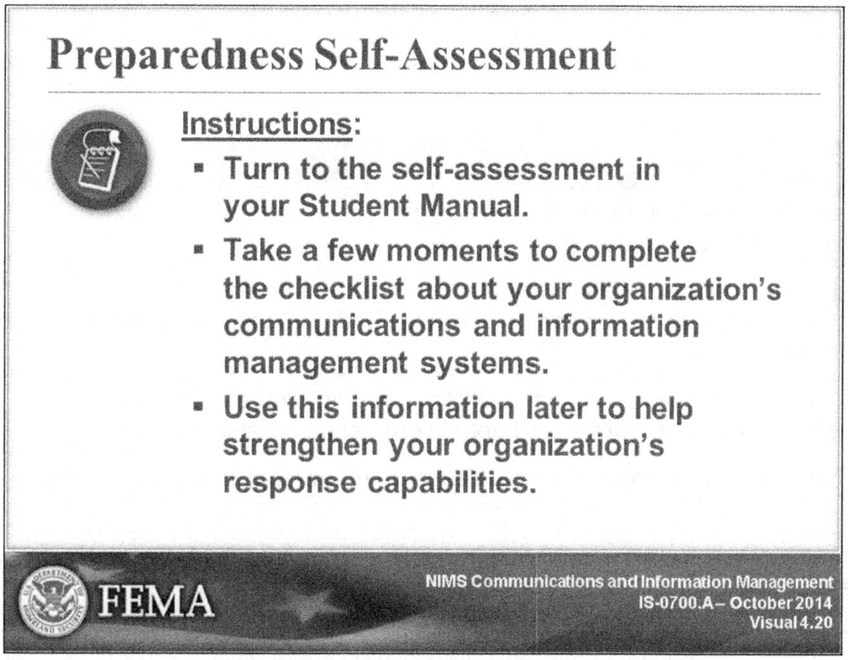

Preparedness Self-Assessment

Instructions:

- Turn to the self-assessment in your Student Manual.
- Take a few moments to complete the checklist about your organization's communications and information management systems.
- Use this information later to help strengthen your organization's response capabilities.

FEMA

NIMS Communications and Information Management
IS-0700.A – October 2014
Visual 4.20

Key Points

Instructions:

- Turn to the self-assessments in your Student Manual.
- Take a few moments to complete the checklists about your organization's communications and information management systems.
- Use this information later to help strengthen your organization's response capabilities.

Self-Assessment: Communications and Information Management Preparedness

Purpose: A common operating picture is established and maintained by the gathering, collating, synthesizing, and disseminating of incident information to all appropriate parties involved in an incident.

Instructions: Complete the following self-assessment to assess your jurisdiction's, agency's, or organization's communications and information management systems preparedness. Use this information to ensure that your jurisdiction, agency, or organization is preparing effectively.

Communications and Information Management Systems	Yes	No
Comply with applicable national standards and are designed to be reliable, portable, scalable, resilient, and redundant.	☐	☐
Allow on-scene and off-scene personnel to have the same information about the incident, including the availability and location of resources and personnel, and the status of requests for assistance.	☐	☐
Specify information that will flow among all stakeholders (including the private sector, critical infrastructure owners and operators, and nongovernmental organizations).	☐	☐
Set policies and procedures for coordination and release of information to the public and media.	☐	☐
Designate the communications systems and platforms that will be used (including technical parameters of all equipment and systems).	☐	☐
Establish protocols for communications that require the use of plain language (and identify exceptions when specialized encryption and tactical language may be used).	☐	☐
Identify procedures and protocols needed to ensure operational and information security.	☐	☐
Specify interoperability and information-sharing arrangements in mutual aid agreements and assistance agreements.	☐	☐
Include periodic training and exercises to ensure that personnel capabilities and limitations of communications plans and systems are addressed before an incident.	☐	☐

Use the space below to make note of action items for your jurisdiction, agency, or organization.

UNIT 5: NIMS RESOURCE MANAGEMENT

Objectives

At the end of this unit, you should be able to:

- Describe the importance of resource management.
- Define the concepts and principles of effective resource management.
- Identify the steps for managing incident resources.

Scope

- Unit Introduction and Objectives
  - Video: What is NIMS Resource Management?
- Principles of Effective Resource Management
  - Standardized Approach
  - Planning
  - Resource Identification and Ordering
  - Effective Resource Management
- Steps for Managing Incident Resources
  - Step #1: Identify Requirements
    - Flow of Requests and Assistance
  - Step #2: Order & Acquire
    - Avoid Bypassing Systems
  - Step #3: Mobilize
    - Mobilization and Demobilization
  - Step #4: Track & Report
  - Step #5: Recover/Demobilize
  - Step #6: Reimburse
  - Step #7: Inventory
    - Identifying and Typing Resources
    - Credentialing
    - Credentialing Process
- Knowledge Review and Summary
- Preparedness Self-Assessment

Unit Introduction and Objectives

Image 5.1

Key Points

This unit presents an overview of the NIMS Resource Management component.

Image 5.2

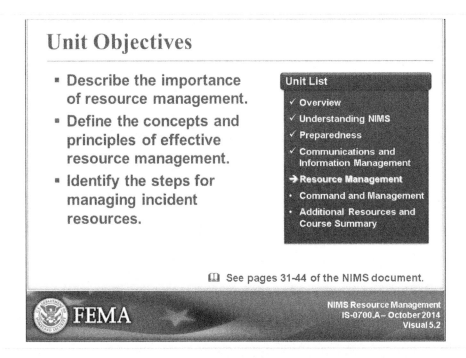

Key Points

At the end of this unit, you should be able to:

- Describe the importance of resource management.
- Define the concepts and principles of effective resource management.
- Identify the steps for managing incident resources.

Refer to pages 31 through 44 of the NIMS document.

Video

Image 5.3

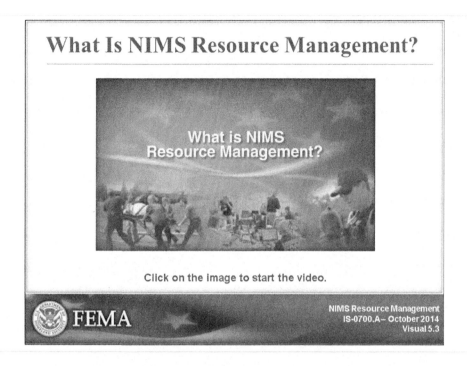

Key Points

This video provides an introduction to the NIMS Resource Management component.

Video Transcript: During an incident, getting the right resources, to the right place, at the right time, can be a matter of life and death. NIMS establishes a standardized approach for managing resources before, during, and after an incident.

Resources include:

- Personnel,
- Equipment,
- Supplies, and
- Facilities.

Prior to an incident, resources are inventoried and categorized by kind and type, including their size, capacity, capability, skills, and other characteristics.

Mutual aid partners exchange information about resource assets and needs. And resource readiness and credentialing are maintained through periodic training and exercises.

When an incident occurs, standardized procedures are used to:

- Identify resource requirements,
- Order and acquire resources, and
- Mobilize resources.

The purpose of tracking and reporting is accountability. Resource accountability helps ensure responder safety and effective use of incident resources. As incident objectives are reached, resources may no longer be necessary. At this point, the recovery and demobilization process begins.

Recovery may involve the rehabilitation, replenishment, disposal, or retrograding of resources, while demobilization is the orderly, safe, and efficient return of an incident resource to its original location and status. And finally, any agreed- upon reimbursement is made.

When disaster strikes, we must be able to take full advantage of all available and qualified resources. In this lesson you will learn how NIMS provides the mechanisms for ensuring that we can be inclusive and integrate resources from all levels of government, the private sector, and nongovernmental organizations.

Principles of Effective Resource Management

Image 5.4

Key Points

NIMS establishes a standardized approach for managing resources before, during, and after an incident. This standardized approach is based on the underlying concepts:

- **Consistency:** Resource management provides a consistent method for identifying, acquiring, allocating, and tracking resources.
- **Standardization:** Resource management includes standardized systems for classifying resources to improve the effectiveness of mutual aid agreements and assistance agreements.
- **Coordination:** Resource management includes coordination to facilitate the integration of resources for optimal benefit.
- **Use:** Resource management planning efforts incorporate use of all available resources from all levels of government, nongovernmental organizations, and the private sector, where appropriate.
- **Information Management:** Resource management integrates communications and information management elements into its organizations, processes, technologies, and decision support.
- **Credentialing:** Resource management includes the use of credentialing criteria that ensure consistent training, licensure, and certification standards.

Image 5.5

Planning

Planning should result in:

- Identification of resource needs.
- Development of alternative strategies to obtain the needed resources.
- Creation of new policies to encourage positioning of resources.
- Identification of conditions that may trigger a specific action.

FEMA

NIMS Resource Management
IS-0700.A – October 2014
Visual 5.5

Key Points

Jurisdictions should work together in advance of an incident to develop plans for identifying, ordering, managing, and employing resources.

The planning process should result in:

- Identification of resource needs based on the threats to and vulnerabilities of the jurisdiction.
- Development of alternative strategies to obtain the needed resources.
- Creation of new policies to encourage positioning of resources.
- Identification of conditions that may trigger a specific action, such as restocking supplies when inventories reach a predetermined minimum.

Image 5.6

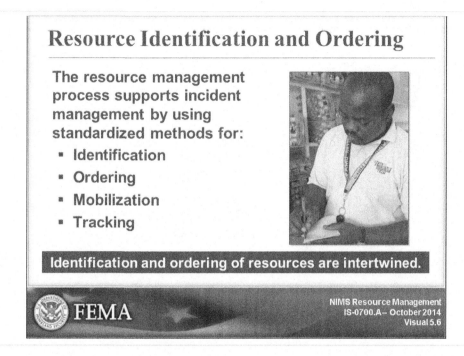

Resource Identification and Ordering

The resource management process supports incident management by using standardized methods for:

- Identification
- Ordering
- Mobilization
- Tracking

Identification and ordering of resources are intertwined.

FEMA

NIMS Resource Management
IS-0700.A – October 2014
Visual 5.6

Key Points

The resource management process uses standardized methods to identify, order, mobilize, and track the resources required to support incident management activities. Identification and ordering of resources are intertwined.

Those with resource management responsibilities perform these tasks either at the request of the Incident Commander or in accordance with planning requirements.

Image 5.7

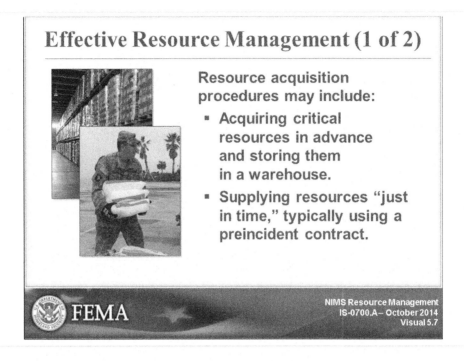

Key Points

Effective resource management includes establishing resource acquisition procedures. It is important to consider the tradeoffs (e.g., shelf life, warehousing costs) and determine the optimal acquisition strategies, including:

- Acquiring critical resources in advance and storing them in a warehouse (i.e., "stockpiling").
- Supplying resources "just in time," typically using a pre-incident contract.

Image 5.8

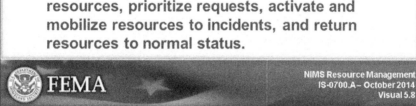

Effective Resource Management (2 of 2)

Effective resource management includes:

- **Management information systems** to collect, update, and process resource data and track the status and location of resources.
- **Standard protocols** to request resources, prioritize requests, activate and mobilize resources to incidents, and return resources to normal status.

FEMA

NIMS Resource Management
IS-0700.A – October 2014
Visual 5.8

Key Points

Effective resource management includes:

- **Systems:** Management information systems collect, update, and process resource data and track the status and location of resources.
  It is critical to have redundant information systems or backup systems to manage resources in the event that the primary system is disrupted or unavailable.
- **Protocols:** Preparedness organizations develop standard protocols to request resources, prioritize requests, activate and mobilize resources to incidents, and return resources to normal status.

Steps for Managing Incident Resources

Image 5.9

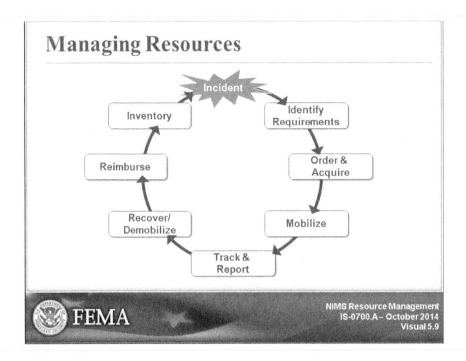

Key Points

The focus of this section of the lesson is on a standardized seven-step cycle for managing resources during an incident.

It is important to remember that preparedness activities must occur on a continual basis to ensure that resources are ready for mobilization.

Image 5.10

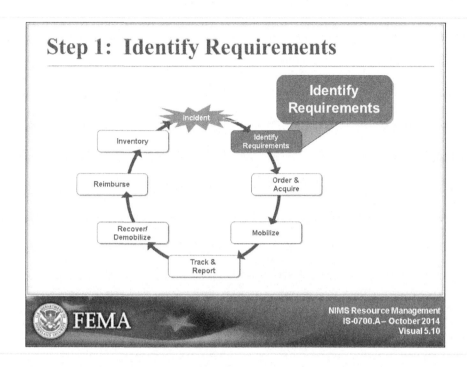

Key Points

When an incident occurs, personnel who have resource management responsibilities should continually identify, refine, and validate resource requirements. This process includes identifying:

- What and how much is needed.
- Where and when it is needed.
- Who will be receiving or using it.

Resource availability and requirements constantly change as the incident evolves. Coordination among all response partners should begin as early as possible, preferably prior to incident response activities.

Image 5.11

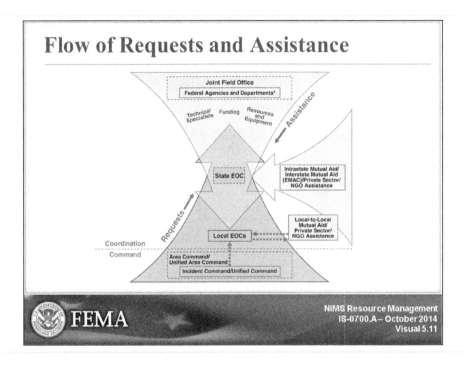

Key Points

This graphic depicts the flow of assistance during large-scale incidents. Present the following information about the flow of requests and assistance:

- The Incident Command/Unified Command identifies resource requirements and communicates needs through the Area Command (if established) to the local Emergency Operations Center (EOC). The local EOC fulfills the need or requests assistance through mutual aid agreements and assistance agreements with private-sector and nongovernmental organizations.
- In most incidents, local resources and local mutual aid agreements and assistance agreements will provide the first line of emergency response and incident management. If the State cannot meet the needs, they may arrange support from another State through an agreement, such as the Emergency Management Assistance Compact (EMAC), or through assistance agreements with nongovernmental organizations.
- If additional resources and/or capabilities are required beyond those available through interstate agreements, the Governor may ask the President for Federal assistance.
- Some Federal agencies (U.S. Coast Guard, Environmental Protection Agency, etc.) have statutory responsibility for response and may coordinate and/or integrate directly with affected jurisdictions.
- Federal assistance may be provided under various Federal authorities. If a Governor requests a disaster declaration, the President will consider the entirety of the situation including damage assessments and needs. The President may declare a major disaster (section 401 of the Robert T. Stafford Disaster Relief and Emergency Assistance Act).
- The Joint Field Office is used to manage Federal assistance (technical specialists, funding, and resources/equipment) that is made available based on the specifics and magnitude of the incident. In instances when an incident is projected to have catastrophic implications (e.g., a major hurricane or flooding), States and/or the Federal Government may position resources in the anticipated incident area.
- In cases where there is time to assess the requirements and plan for a catastrophic incident, the

Federal response will be coordinated with State, tribal, and local jurisdictions, and the pre-positioning of Federal assets will be tailored to address the specific situation.

Image 5.12

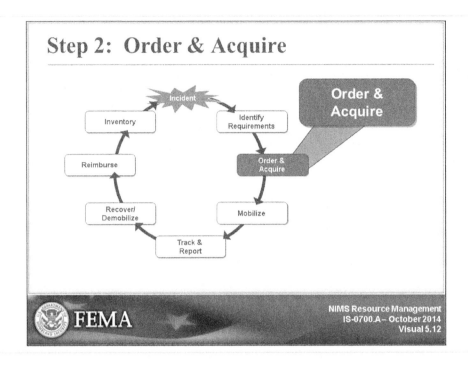

Key Points

Standardized resource-ordering procedures are used when requests for resources cannot be fulfilled locally. Typically, these requests are forwarded first to an adjacent locality or substate region and then to the State.

Decisions about resource allocation are based on organization or agency protocol and possibly the resource demands of other incidents.

Mutual aid and assistance resources will be mobilized only with the consent of the jurisdiction that is being asked to provide the requested resources. Discrepancies between requested resources and those available for delivery must be communicated to the requestor.

Image 5.13

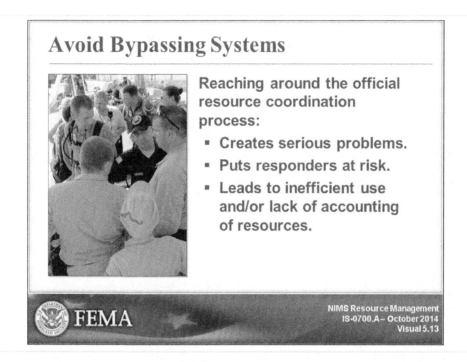

Key Points

Those responsible for managing resources, including public officials, should recognize that reaching around the official resource coordination process within the Multiagency Coordination System supporting the incident(s) creates serious problems.

Requests from outside the established system can put responders at risk, and at best typically lead to inefficient use and/or lack of accounting of resources.

Image 5.14

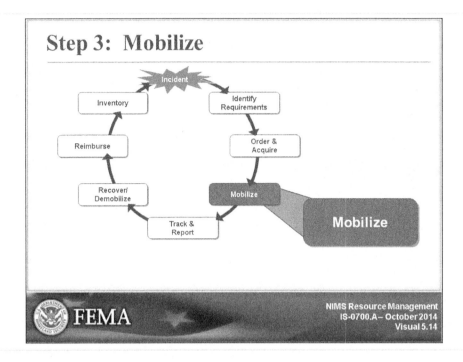

Key Points

Incident resources mobilize as soon as they are notified through established channels. Mobilization notifications should include:

- The date, time, and place of departure.
- Mode of transportation to the incident.
- Estimated date and time of arrival.
- Reporting location (address, contact name, and phone number).
- Anticipated incident assignment.
- Anticipated duration of deployment.
- Resource order number.
- Incident number.
- Applicable cost and funding codes.

When resources arrive on scene, they must be formally checked in.

Image 5.15

Mobilization and Demobilization

Demobilization planning:

- Begins at the same time as mobilization.
- Facilitates accountability and efficiency.
- Occurs in the Planning Section.

 FEMA

NIMS Resource Management
IS-0700.A – October 2014
Visual 5.15

Key Points

Managers should plan and prepare for the demobilization process at the same time that they begin the resource mobilization process.

Early planning for demobilization facilitates accountability and makes the logistical management of resources as efficient as possible—in terms of both costs and time of delivery.

The Demobilization Unit in the Planning Section develops an Incident Demobilization Plan containing specific demobilization instructions.

Image 5.16

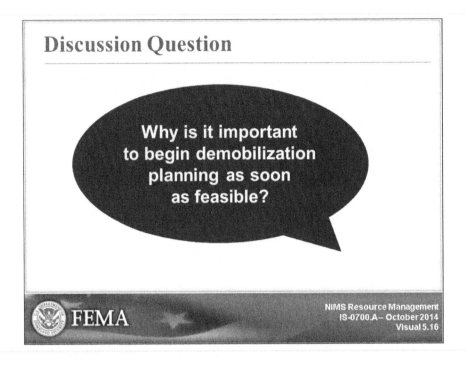

Key Points

Answer the following discussion question:

- **Why is it important to begin demobilization planning as soon as feasible?**

Image 5.17

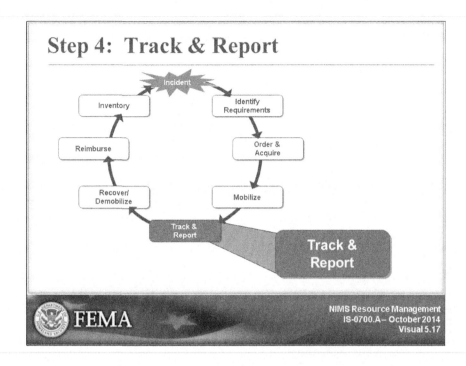

Key Points

Resource tracking is a standardized, integrated process conducted prior to, during, and after an incident to:

- Provide a clear picture of where resources are located.
- Help staff prepare to receive resources.
- Protect the safety and security of personnel, equipment, and supplies.
- Enable resource coordination and movement.

Resources are tracked using established procedures continuously from mobilization through demobilization.

Image 5.18

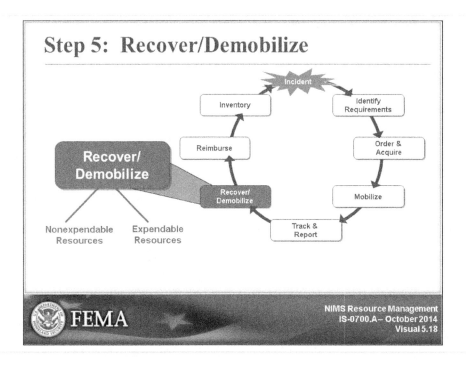

Key Points

- Recovery involves the final disposition of all resources, including those located at the incident site and at fixed facilities. During this process, resources are rehabilitated, replenished, disposed of, and/or retrograded.

- Demobilization is the orderly, safe, and efficient return of an incident resource to its original location and status. As stated earlier, demobilization planning should begin as soon as possible to facilitate accountability of the resources. During demobilization, the Incident Command and Multiagency Coordination System elements coordinate to prioritize critical resource needs and reassign resources (if necessary).

- Nonexpendable Resources (such as personnel, firetrucks, and durable equipment) are fully accounted for both during the incident and when they are returned to the providing organization. The organization then restores the resources to full functional capability and readies them for the next mobilization. Broken or lost items should be replaced through the appropriate resupply process, by the organization with invoicing responsibility for the incident, or as defined in existing agreements. It is critical that fixed-facility resources also be restored to their full functional capability in order to ensure readiness for the next mobilization. In the case of human resources, such as Incident Management Teams, adequate rest and recuperation time and facilities should be provided. Important occupational health and mental health issues should also be addressed, including monitoring the immediate and long-term effects of the incident (chronic and acute) on emergency management/response personnel.

- Expendable Resources (such as water, food, fuel, and other one-time-use supplies) must be fully accounted for. The incident management organization bears the costs of expendable resources, as authorized in financial agreements executed by preparedness organizations. Restocking occurs at the point from which a resource was issued. Returned resources that are not in restorable condition (whether expendable or nonexpendable) must be declared as excess according to established regulations and policies of the controlling jurisdiction, agency, or organization. Waste management is of special note in the process of recovering resources, as resources that require special handling and disposition (e.g., biological waste and contaminated supplies, debris, and equipment) are handled according to established regulations and policies.

Image 5.19

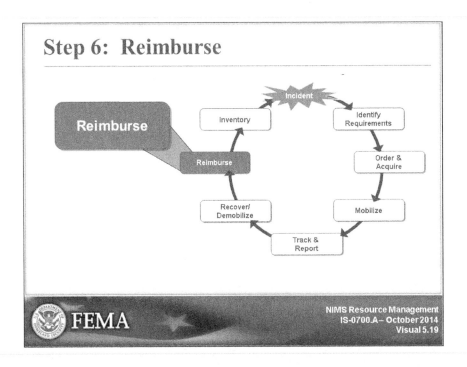

Key Points

Reimbursement provides a mechanism to recoup funds expended for incident-specific activities. Consideration should be given to reimbursement agreements prior to an incident. Processes for reimbursement play an important role in establishing and maintaining the readiness of resources.

Preparedness plans, mutual aid agreements, and assistance agreements should specify reimbursement terms and arrangements for:

- Collecting bills and documentation.
- Validating costs against the scope of the work.
- Ensuring that proper authorities are secured.
- Using proper procedures/forms and accessing any reimbursement software programs.

Image 5.20

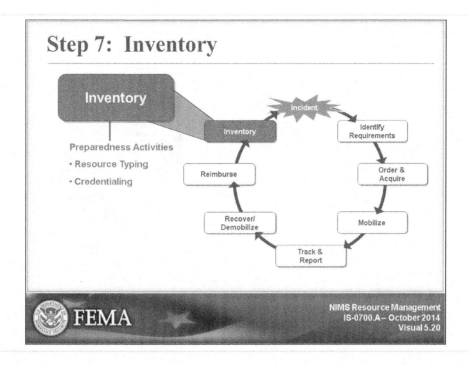

Key Points

Resource management uses various resource inventory systems to assess the availability of assets provided by jurisdictions.

Preparedness organizations should inventory and maintain current data on their available resources. The data are then made available to communications/dispatch centers, Emergency Operations Centers, and other organizations within the Multiagency Coordination System.

Resources identified within an inventory system are not an indication of automatic availability. The jurisdiction and/or owner of the resources has the final determination on availability.

Image 5.21

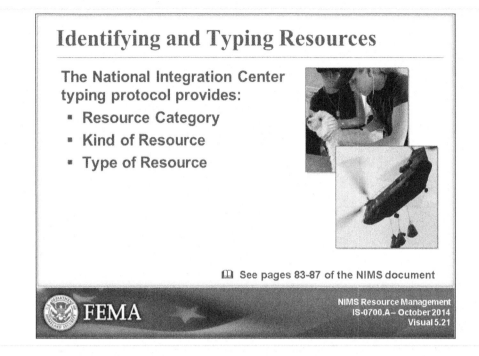

Key Points

Resource typing is categorizing, by capability, the resources requested, deployed, and used in incidents. The National Integration Center typing protocol provides incident managers the following information:

- **Resource Category:** Identifies the function for which a resource would be most useful.
- **Kind of Resource:** Describes what the resource is (for example: medic, firefighter, Planning Section Chief, helicopter, ambulance, combustible gas indicator, bulldozer).
- **Type of Resource:** Describes the size, capability, and staffing qualifications of a specific kind of resource.

Resource typing must be a continuous process based on measurable standards.

Refer to Annex A of the NIMS document for an example of resource typing. Annex A begins on page 83.

Image 5.22

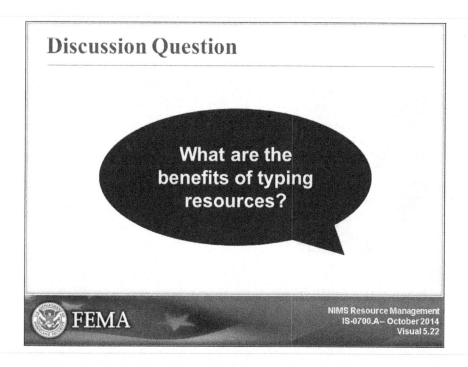

Key Points

Answer the following discussion question:

- **What are the benefits of typing resources?**

Image 5.23

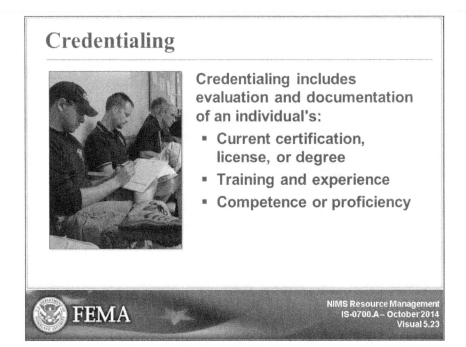

Key Points

The credentialing process involves an objective evaluation and documentation of an individual's:

- Current certification, license, or degree,
- Training and experience, and
- Competence or proficiency.

Credentialing personnel ensures that they meet nationally accepted standards and are able to perform specific tasks under specific conditions. Credentialing is separate from badging, which takes place at the incident site in order to control access.

Image 5.24

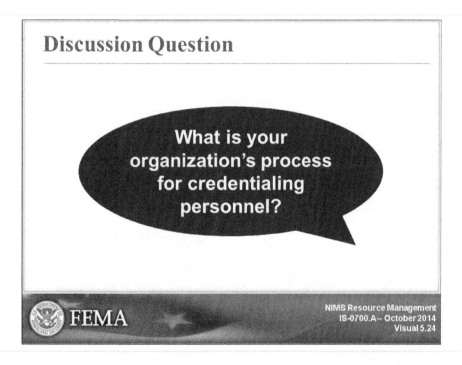

Key Points

Answer the following discussion question:

- **What is your organization's process for credentialing personnel?**

Image 5.25

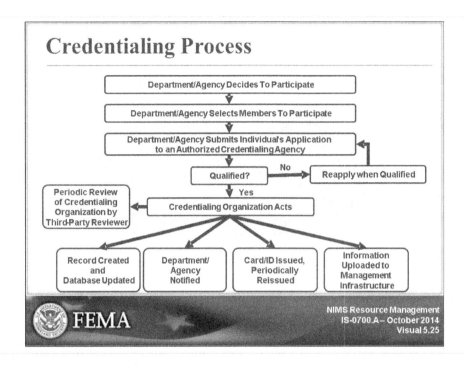

Key Points

The visual illustrates the process, as recommended by the National Integration Center, for credentialing under NIMS.

The process begins with the department/agency deciding to participate in the credentialing effort. Next the department/agency selects members to participate in the credentialing effort.

The department/agency submits each individual's application to an authorized credentialing agency. That credentialing agency determines if the individual is qualified for the applied-for credential(s).

If the individual is found not qualified, he/she can reapply when qualified.

If the individual is found qualified, the credentialing agency acts as follows:

- Creates a record and updates the database.
- Issues a card/ID (and periodically reissues the card/ID as appropriate).
- Notifies the department/agency.
- Uploads the information to the management infrastructure.

The credentialing organization undergoes periodic review by a third-party reviewer.

Knowledge Review and Summary

Image 5.26

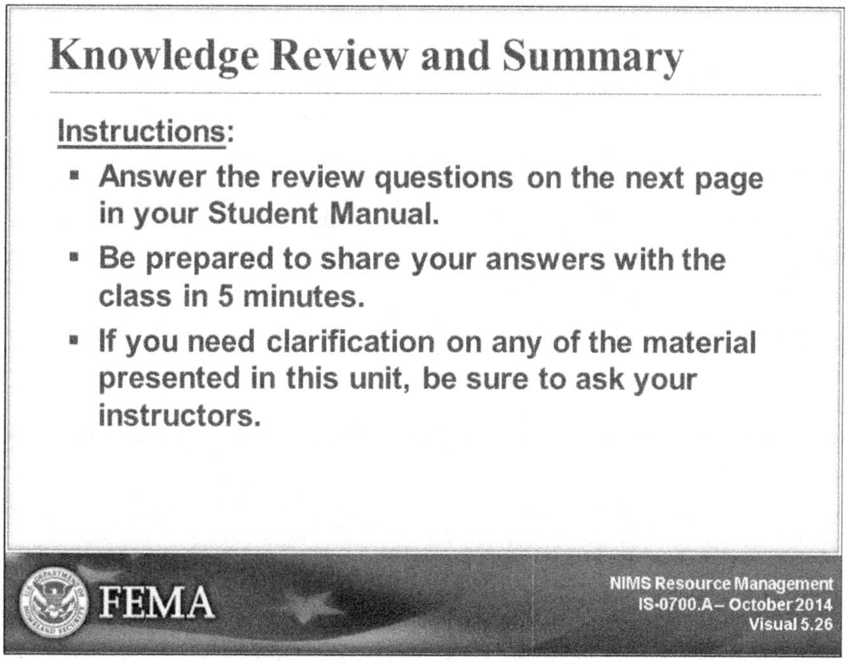

Knowledge Review and Summary

Instructions:

- Answer the review questions on the next page in your Student Manual.
- Be prepared to share your answers with the class in 5 minutes.
- If you need clarification on any of the material presented in this unit, be sure to ask your instructors.

 FEMA

NIMS Resource Management
IS-0700.A – October 2014
Visual 5.26

Key Points

Instructions:

- Answer the review questions on the next page.
- Be prepared to share your answers with the class in 5 minutes.
- If you need clarification on any of the material presented in this unit, ask your instructors.

Unit 5: Knowledge Review

1. When should planning for the demobilization process begin?

2. What is the process used to rehabilitate, replenish, dispose of, and/or retrograde resources?

3. Fill in the blanks below. The credentialing process involves an objective evaluation and documentation of an individual's:
   - Current certification, license, or degree,
   - Training and experience, and
   - _____

4. Use the space below to make note of any questions you have about the material covered in this unit.

Preparedness Self-Assessment

Image 5.27

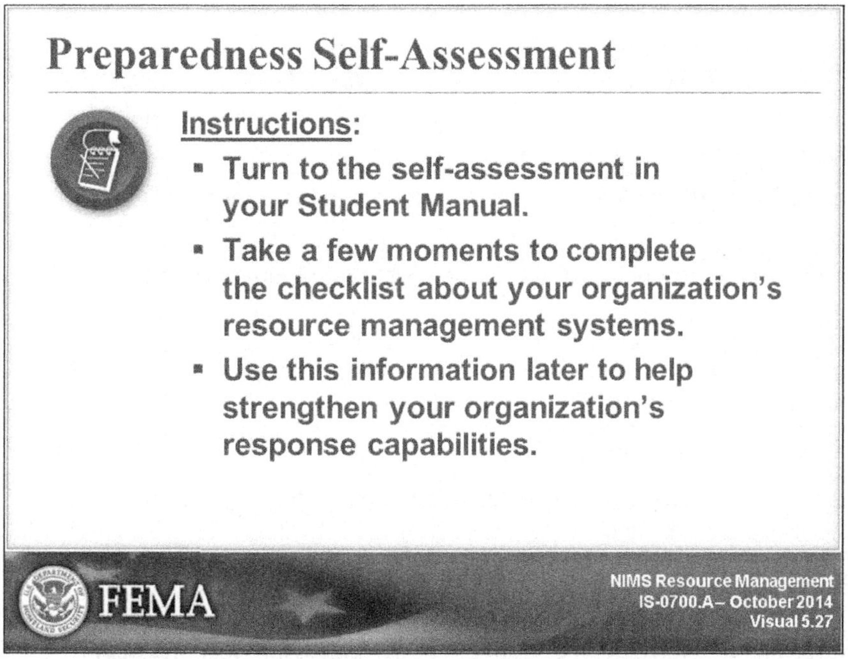

Preparedness Self-Assessment

Instructions:

- **Turn to the self-assessment in your Student Manual.**
- **Take a few moments to complete the checklist about your organization's resource management systems.**
- **Use this information later to help strengthen your organization's response capabilities.**

 FEMA

NIMS Resource Management
IS-0700.A – October 2014
Visual 5.27

Key Points

Instructions:

- Turn to the self-assessments in your Student Manual.
- Take a few moments to complete the checklists about your organization's communications and information management systems.
- Use this information later to help strengthen your organization's response capabilities.

Self-Assessment: Resource Management Preparedness

Instructions: Complete the following self-assessment to assess your jurisdiction's, agency's, or organization's resource management systems preparedness. Use this information to ensure that your jurisdiction, agency, or organization is preparing effectively.

My jurisdiction, agency, or organization has	Yes	No
A resource management plan that identifies resource needs based on the threats and vulnerabilities of the jurisdiction.	☐	☐
Procedures for inventorying and maintaining current data on available resources (pre-incident).	☐	☐
A process for credentialing personnel based upon objective evaluation measures.	☐	☐
Procedures for using NIMS typing standards.	☐	☐
Mutual aid agreements and assistance agreements that address resource management procedures including reimbursement terms and procedures.	☐	☐
Protocols and procedures for positioning of resources.	☐	☐
Identified conditions that may trigger a specific action, such as restocking supplies when inventories reach a predetermined minimum.	☐	☐
Management information systems to collect data and track the status and location of resources.	☐	☐
Redundant information systems or backup systems to manage resources in the event that the primary system is disrupted or unavailable.	☐	☐
Established procedures and protocols for identifying resource requirements, requesting resources, prioritizing requests, activating and mobilizing resources to incidents, and returning resources to normal status.	☐	☐
Procedures for ensuring that all tactical resources check in at an incident site and report any change in status.	☐	☐
Standard planning formats and procedures for demobilizing resources.	☐	☐

Use the space below to make note of action items for your jurisdiction, agency, or organization.

UNIT 6: NIMS COMMAND AND MANAGEMENT

Objectives

At the end of this unit, you should be able to define the concepts and principles related to the following Command and Management elements:

- Incident Command System
- Multiagency Coordination Systems
- Public Information

Scope

- Unit Introduction and Objectives
- Introduction to NIMS Command and Management
    - Command and Management Elements
    - Video: What Is NIMS Command and Management?
    - Understanding Command and Coordination
- Incident Command System
    - What Is ICS?
    - ICS Features
    - Incident Command Functions
    - Incident Commander
    - Incident Command Post
    - Command Staff
    - General Staff
    - Unified Command
        - Unified Command Benefits
        - Single vs. Unified Command
    - Area Command
    - Incident Management Teams
- Multiagency Coordination Systems
    - Multiagency Support and Coordination
    - A System... Not a Facility
    - Emergency Operations Center (EOC)
    - On-Scene and Off-Scene Multiagency Coordination
- Public Information
    - Managing Public Information
    - Joint Information Center (JIC)
    - Speaking with One Voice
    - Joint Information System (JIS)
- Knowledge Check and Summary
- Preparedness Self-Assessment

Unit Introduction and Objectives

Image 6.1

Key Points

This unit presents an overview of the NIMS Command and Management component.

Image 6.2

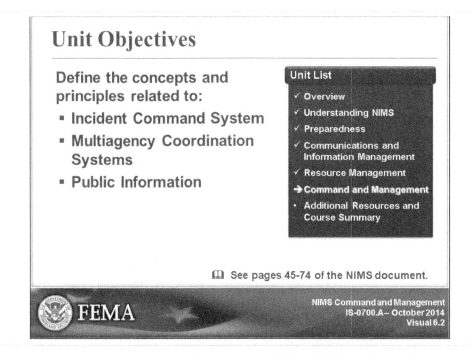

Key Points

At the end of this unit, you should be able to define the concepts and principles related to the following Command and Management elements:

- Incident Command System
- Multiagency Coordination Systems
- Public Information

This unit summarizes the information presented in Component IV: Command and Management, including:

- Incident Command System
- Multiagency Coordination Systems
- Public Information
- Relationships Among Command and Management Elements

Refer to pages 45 through 74 of the NIMS document.

Introduction to NIMS Command and Management

Image 6.3

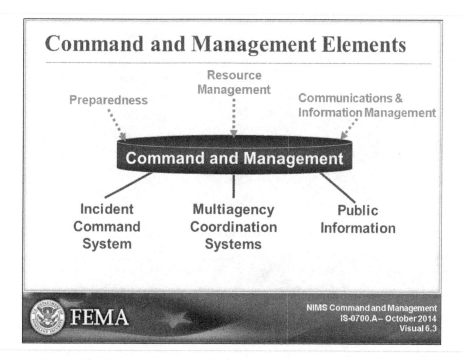

Key Points

This unit is divided into three sections covering each of the Command and Management elements:

- Incident Command System
- Multiagency Coordination Systems
- Public Information

The NIMS Command and Management component facilitates incident management by building upon all of the components covered in the previous lessons.

Image 6.4

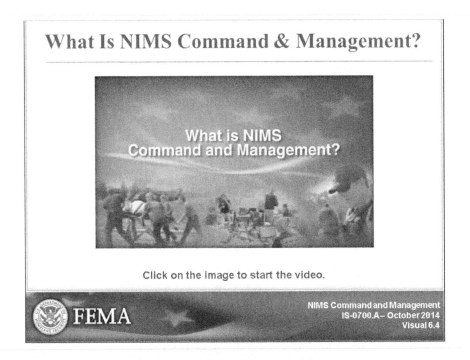

Key Points

The video provides an introduction to the NIMS Command and Management component.

Video Transcript: The NIMS components of Preparedness, Communications and Information Management, and Resource Management provide a framework for effective management during incident response. Next, we'll cover the fundamental elements of incident management including: Incident Command System, Multiagency Coordination Systems, and Public Information. Together, these elements comprise the NIMS Command and Management component. The Incident Command System, or ICS, is a standardized, on-scene, all-hazard incident management concept. ICS allows its users to adopt an integrated organizational structure to match the complexities and demands of incidents.

NIMS is best summed up by Craig Fugate: ". . .When we fail to work as a team, we fail our citizens and what NIMS is, is a system to provide a framework for all of the team to work together towards common goals."

As an incident becomes more complex, multiagency coordination becomes increasingly important. Multiagency coordination is a process that allows all levels of government and all disciplines to work together more efficiently and effectively. Multiagency coordination is accomplished through a comprehensive system of elements. These elements include facilities, equipment, personnel, procedures, and communications. Emergency Operations Centers and Multiagency Coordination Groups are just two examples of coordination elements.

The final Command and Management element is Public Information. Public Information includes processes, procedures, and organizational structures required to gather, verify, coordinate, and disseminate information— information that is essential for lifesaving response and community recovery.

Image 6.5

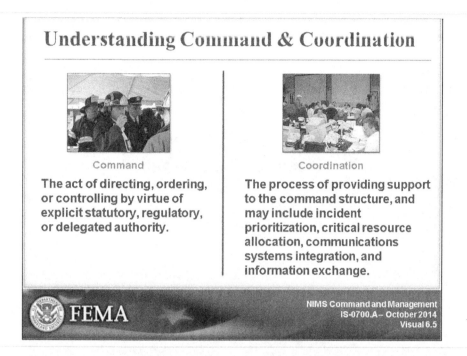

Key Points

This unit presents information on command and coordination. Both elements are essential to ensuring a successful response. Remind the participants that:

- **Command** is the act of directing, ordering, or controlling by virtue of explicit statutory, regulatory, or delegated authority at the field level.
- **Coordination** is the process of providing support to the command structure and may include incident prioritization, critical resource allocation, communications systems integration, and information exchange.

Incident Command System

Image 6.6

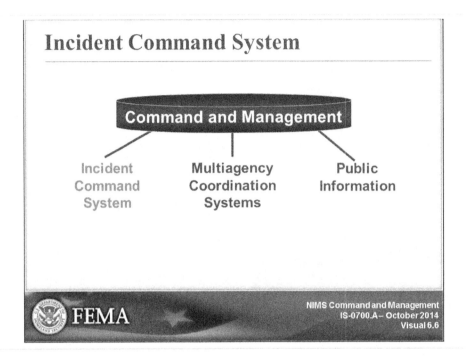

Key Points

- The first Command and Management element is the Incident Command System (ICS).
- This unit reviews the key ICS concepts and terminology used within NIMS and is not a substitute for comprehensive ICS training. Additional information on ICS training requirements is available at the National Integration Center Web site.

Image 6.7

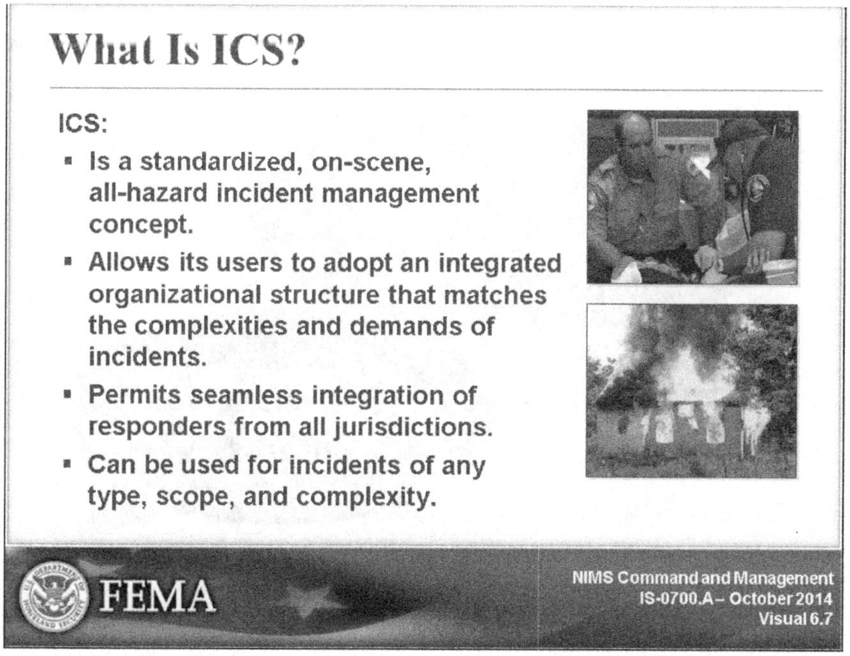

Key Points

ICS is a standardized, on-scene, all-hazards incident management approach that:

- Allows for the integration of facilities, equipment, personnel, procedures, and communications operating within a common organizational structure.
- Enables a coordinated response among various jurisdictions and functional agencies, both public and private.
- Establishes common processes for planning and managing resources.

By using management best practices, ICS helps to ensure:

- The safety of responders and others.
- The achievement of tactical objectives.
- The efficient use of resources.

NIMS prompts the use of ICS for every incident or scheduled event. Using ICS on all incidents helps hone and maintain skills needed for the large-scale incidents.

Image 6.8

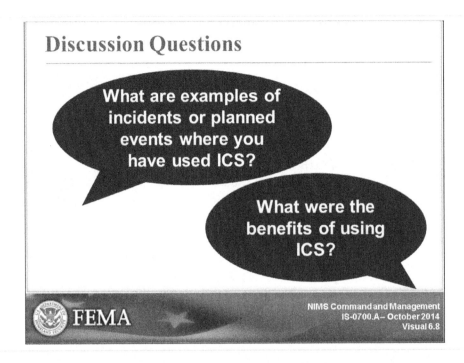

Key Points

Answer the following discussion questions:

- **What are examples of incidents or planned events where you have used ICS?**

- **What were the benefits of using ICS?**

Image 6.9

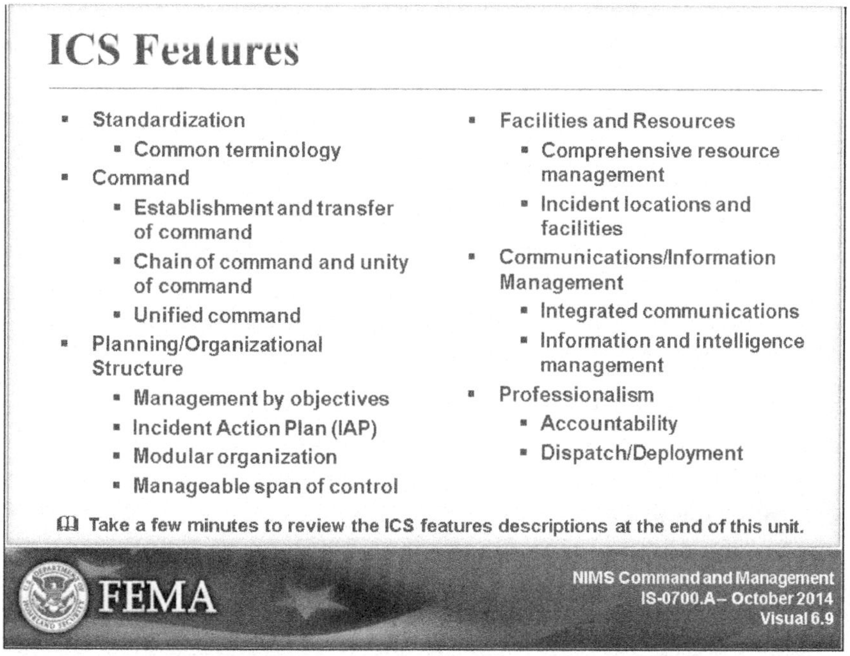

ICS Features

- Standardization
  - Common terminology
- Command
  - Establishment and transfer of command
  - Chain of command and unity of command
  - Unified command
- Planning/Organizational Structure
  - Management by objectives
  - Incident Action Plan (IAP)
  - Modular organization
  - Manageable span of control

- Facilities and Resources
  - Comprehensive resource management
  - Incident locations and facilities
- Communications/Information Management
  - Integrated communications
  - Information and intelligence management
- Professionalism
  - Accountability
  - Dispatch/Deployment

📖 Take a few minutes to review the ICS features descriptions at the end of this unit.

FEMA

NIMS Command and Management
IS-0700.A – October 2014
Visual 6.9

Key Points

ICS is based on 14 proven management characteristics that contribute to the strength and efficiency of the overall system. Refer the participants to the reference materials about the 14 features of ICS located at the end of this unit.

Image 6.10

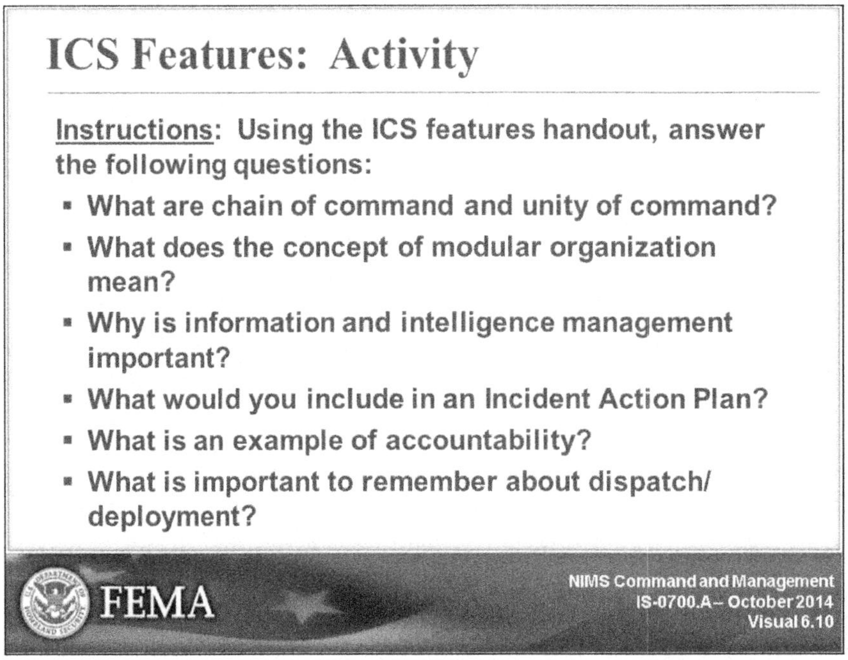

ICS Features: Activity

Instructions: Using the ICS features handout, answer the following questions:

- What are chain of command and unity of command?
- What does the concept of modular organization mean?
- Why is information and intelligence management important?
- What would you include in an Incident Action Plan?
- What is an example of accountability?
- What is important to remember about dispatch/deployment?

 FEMA

NIMS Command and Management
IS-0700.A – October 2014
Visual 6.10

Key Points

Refer to the descriptions of the 14 features on the handout at the end of this unit. Next, ask for volunteers to answer each of the following questions:

- **What are chain of command and unity of command?**

- **What does the concept of modular organization mean?**

- **Why is information and intelligence management important?**

- **What would you include in an Incident Action Plan?**

- **What is an example of accountability?**

- **What is important to remember about dispatch/deployment?**

Image 6.11

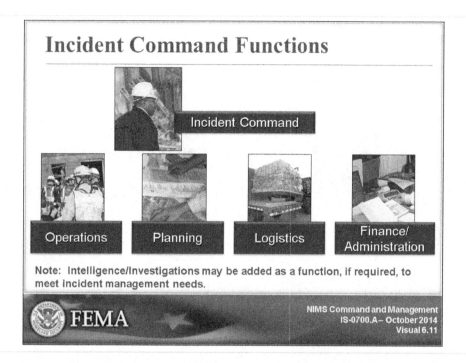

Key Points

- Every incident requires that certain management functions be performed. The problem must be identified and assessed, a plan to deal with it developed and implemented, and the necessary resources procured and paid for.
- Regardless of the size of the incident, these management functions still will apply.
- There are five major management functions that are the foundation upon which the ICS organization develops. These functions include:
  - **Incident Command:** Sets the incident objectives, strategies, and priorities and has overall responsibility for the incident.
  - **Operations:** Conducts operations to reach the incident objectives. Establishes the tactics and directs all operational resources.
  - **Planning:** Supports the incident action planning process by tracking resources, collecting/analyzing information, and maintaining documentation.
  - **Logistics:** Provides resources and needed services to support the achievement of the incident objectives.
  - **Finance & Administration:** Monitors costs related to the incident. Provides purchasing and accounting support.

ICS allows its users to adopt an integrated organizational structure to match the complexities and demands of single or multiple incidents.

Image 6.12

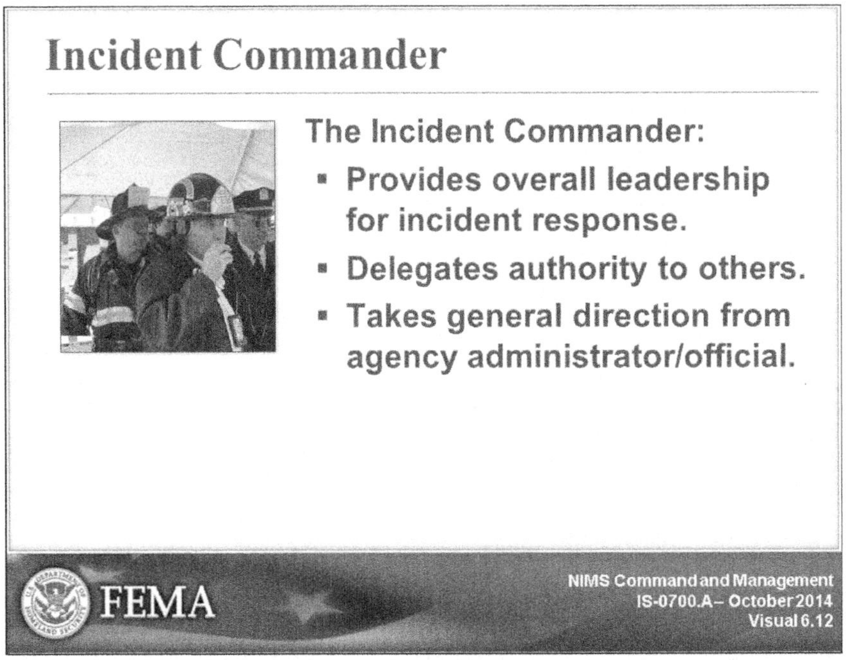

Incident Commander

The Incident Commander:

- Provides overall leadership for incident response.
- Delegates authority to others.
- Takes general direction from agency administrator/official.

FEMA

NIMS Command and Management
IS-0700.A – October 2014
Visual 6.12

Key Points

- When an incident occurs within a single jurisdiction and there is no jurisdictional or functional agency overlap, a single Incident Commander is designated with overall incident management responsibility by the appropriate jurisdictional authority. The designated Incident Commander develops the incident objectives that direct all subsequent incident action planning. The Incident Commander approves the Incident Action Plan and the resources to be ordered or released.
- The Incident Commander has overall responsibility for managing the incident by establishing objectives, planning strategies, and implementing tactics.
- The Incident Commander is the only position that is always staffed in ICS applications. On small incidents and events, one person, the Incident Commander, may accomplish all management functions.
- The Incident Commander has overall authority and responsibility for conducting incident operations and is responsible for the management of all incident operations at the incident site. The Incident Commander must:
  - Have clear authority and know agency policy.
  - Ensure incident safety.
  - Establish the Incident Command Post.
  - Set priorities, and determine incident objectives and strategies to be followed.
  - Establish the Incident Command System organization needed to manage the incident.
  - Approve the Incident Action Plan.
  - Coordinate Command and General Staff activities.
  - Approve resource requests and use of volunteers and auxiliary personnel.
  - Order demobilization as needed.
  - Ensure after-action reports are completed.
  - Authorize information released to the media.

Image 6.13

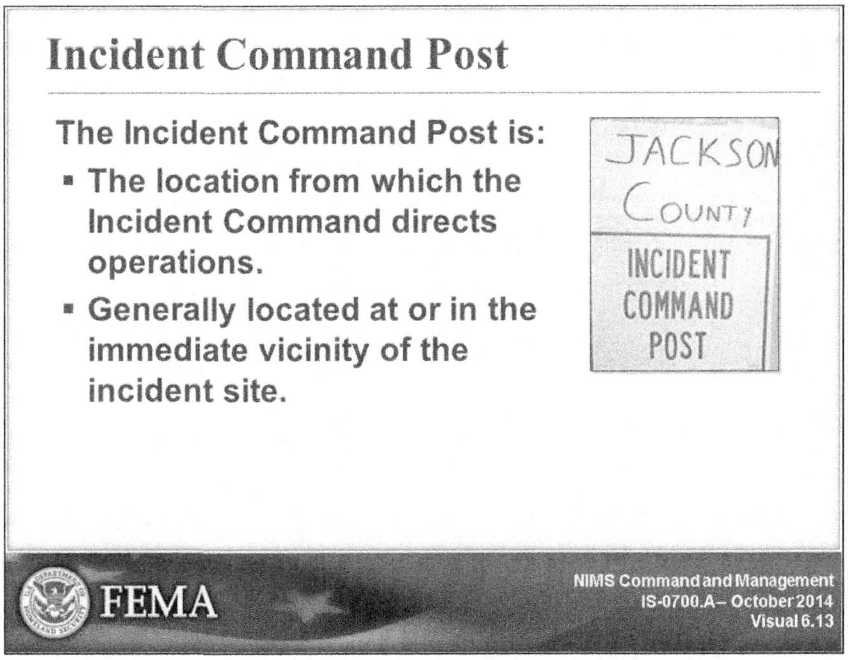

Key Points

The incident Command and Management organization is located at the Incident Command Post (ICP). Incident Command directs operations from the ICP, which is generally located at or in the immediate vicinity of the incident site. Typically, one ICP is established for each incident.

As emergency management/response personnel deploy, they must, regardless of agency affiliation, report to and check in at the designated location and receive an assignment in accordance with the established procedures.

Image 6.14

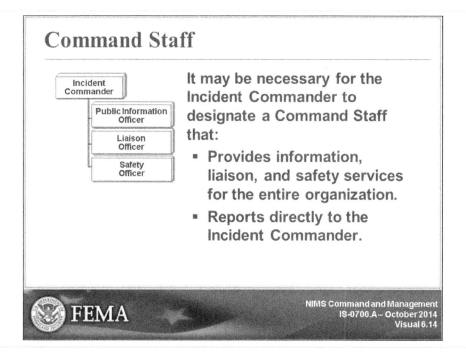

Key Points

In an Incident Command organization, the Command Staff typically includes the following personnel:

- The **Public Information Officer** is responsible for interfacing with the public and media and/or with other agencies with incident-related information requirements.
- The **Safety Officer** monitors incident operations and advises the Incident Commander/Unified Command on all matters relating to operational safety, including the health and safety of emergency responder personnel.
- The **Liaison Officer** is the point of contact for representatives of other governmental agencies, nongovernmental organizations, and the private sector.

Additional Command Staff positions may be added depending upon incident needs and requirements.

Image 6.15

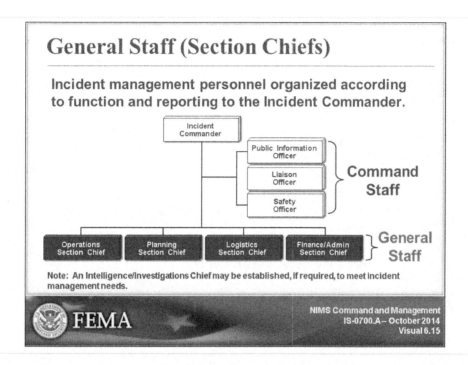

Key Points

The General Staff includes a group of incident management personnel organized according to function and reporting to the Incident Commander. Typically, the General Staff consists of the Operations Section Chief, Planning Section Chief, Logistics Section Chief, and Finance/Administration Section Chief.

Reference materials at the end of this unit in their Student Manuals for more information about each position within the Command and General Staffs.

Image 6.16

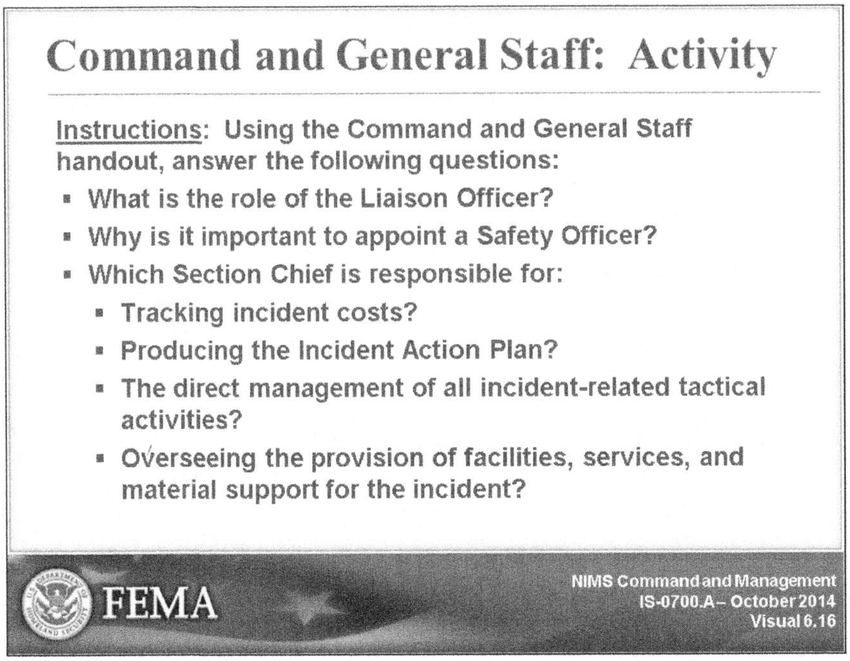

Command and General Staff: Activity

Instructions: Using the Command and General Staff handout, answer the following questions:

- What is the role of the Liaison Officer?
- Why is it important to appoint a Safety Officer?
- Which Section Chief is responsible for:
  - Tracking incident costs?
  - Producing the Incident Action Plan?
  - The direct management of all incident-related tactical activities?
  - Overseeing the provision of facilities, services, and material support for the incident?

 **FEMA**

NIMS Command and Management
IS-0700.A – October 2014
Visual 6.16

Key Points

Refer to the descriptions of the Command and General Staff on the handout at the end of this unit. Next, ask for volunteers to answer each of the following questions:

- **What is the role of the Liaison Officer?**

- **Why is it important to appoint a Safety Officer?**

- **Which Section Chief is responsible for:**
  - **Tracking incident costs?**

  - **Producing the Incident Action Plan?**

  - **The direct management of all incident-related tactical activities?**

  - **Overseeing the provision of facilities, services, and material support for the incident?**

Image 6.17

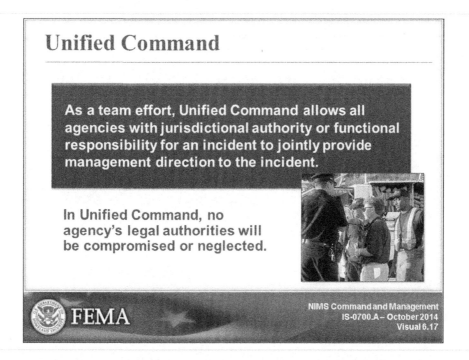

Key Points

- Early in the development of ICS, it was recognized that many incidents crossed jurisdictional boundaries or the limits of individual agency functional responsibility.
- As a team effort, Unified Command allows all agencies with jurisdictional authority or functional responsibility for an incident to jointly provide management direction to the incident.
- NIMS encourages the use of Unified Command when appropriate.

This excerpt is from the following longer quote from the NIMS document:

"Unified Command is an important element in multijurisdictional or multiagency incident management. It provides guidelines to enable agencies with different legal, geographic, and functional responsibilities to coordinate, plan, and interact effectively. As a team effort, Unified Command allows all agencies with jurisdictional authority or functional responsibility for the incident to jointly provide management direction to an incident through a common set of incident objectives and strategies and a single Incident Action Plan. Each participating agency maintains its authority, responsibility, or accountability."

Image 6.18

Unified Command Benefits

- A shared understanding of priorities and restrictions.
- A single set of incident objectives.
- Collaborative strategies.
- Improved internal and external information flow.
- Less duplication of efforts.
- Better resource utilization.

FEMA

NIMS Command and Management
IS-0700.A – October 2014
Visual 6.18

Key Points

In multijurisdictional or multiagency incident management, Unified Command offers the following advantages:

- A single set of objectives is developed for the entire incident.
- A collective "team" approach is used to develop strategies to achieve incident objectives.
- Information flow and coordination are improved between all jurisdictions and agencies involved in the incident.
- All agencies with responsibility for the incident have an understanding of joint priorities and restrictions.
- No agency's legal authorities are compromised or neglected.
- The combined efforts of all agencies are optimized as they perform their respective assignments under a single Incident Action Plan.

Image 6.19

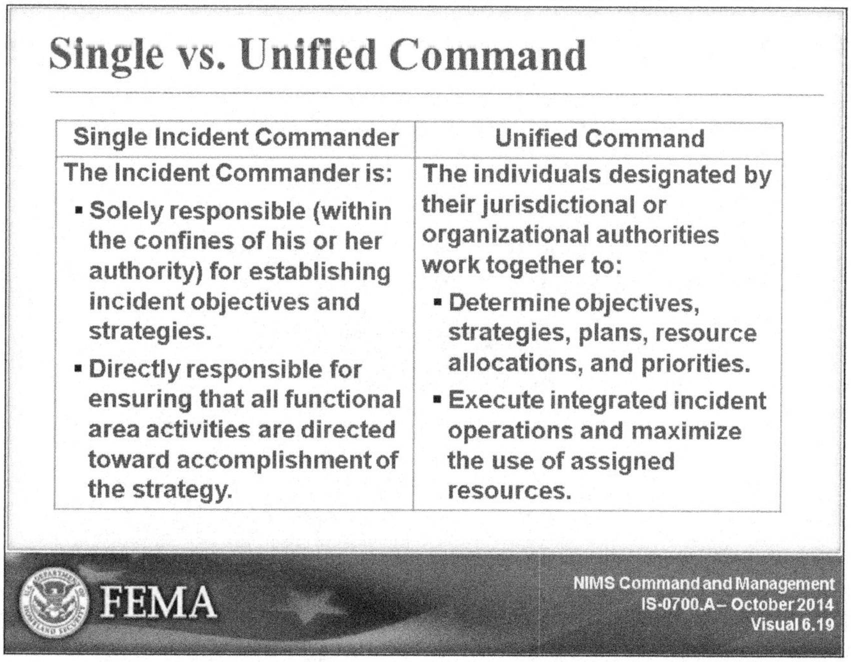

Single vs. Unified Command

Single Incident Commander	Unified Command
The Incident Commander is: • Solely responsible (within the confines of his or her authority) for establishing incident objectives and strategies. • Directly responsible for ensuring that all functional area activities are directed toward accomplishment of the strategy.	The individuals designated by their jurisdictional or organizational authorities work together to: • Determine objectives, strategies, plans, resource allocations, and priorities. • Execute integrated incident operations and maximize the use of assigned resources.

FEMA

NIMS Command and Management
IS-0700.A – October 2014
Visual 6.19

Key Points

Note the following differences between single and unified command structures.

- **Single Incident Commander:** The Incident Commander is:
  - Solely responsible (within the confines of his or her authority) for establishing incident objectives and strategies.
  - Directly responsible for ensuring that all functional area activities are directed toward accomplishment of the strategy.
- **Unified Command:** The individuals designated by their jurisdictional or organizational authorities (or by departments within a single jurisdiction) work together to:
  - Determine objectives, strategies, plans, resource allocations, and priorities.
  - Execute integrated incident operations and maximize the use of assigned resources.

Image 6.20

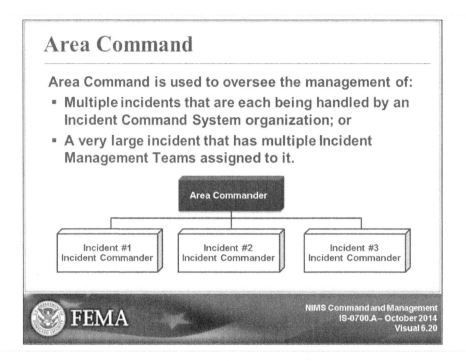

Key Points

- Area Command is used when there are a number of incidents generally in the same area and often of the same kind. Examples include two or more hazardous materials spills, fires, etc. Often these kinds of incidents will vie for the same resources.
- When an incident expands to a large geographic area, the agency officials may choose to divide the incident into smaller pieces, called zones, each of which will be managed by an Incident Management Team (IMT).
- When incidents are of different kinds and/or do not have similar resource demands, they will usually be handled as separate incidents or will be coordinated through an Emergency Operations Center (EOC).

The use of an Area Command makes the jobs of Incident Commanders and agency officials easier for the following reasons:

- Much of the cross-incident coordination typically performed by each Incident Commander is accomplished at the Area Command level. Using an Area Command allows the Incident Commanders and their IMTs to focus attention on their incident objectives, strategies, and tactics.
- Area Command sets priorities between incidents and ensures efficient resource use. Critical resources are allocated by the overall priorities established by the agency officials. Competition among incidents for critical resources is avoided. Often, agency dispatchers will recognize cross-incident coordination problems first.
- Area Command ensures that agency policies, priorities, constraints, and guidance are being made known to the Incident Commanders and implemented consistently across incidents.
- Area Command also reduces the workload of Executives/Senior Officials, especially if there are multiple incidents going on at the same time.

Image 6.21

Area Command: Primary Functions

- Provide agency or jurisdictional authority for assigned incidents.
- Ensure a clear understanding of agency expectations, intentions, and constraints.
- Establish critical resource use priorities between various incidents.
- Ensure that Incident Management Team personnel assignments and organizations are appropriate.
- Maintain contact with officials in charge, and other agencies and groups.
- Coordinate the demobilization or reassignment of resources between assigned incidents.

FEMA

NIMS Command and Management
IS-0700.A – October 2014
Visual 6.21

Key Points

The Area Command is designed to ensure the effective management of assigned incidents. To do this, the Area Commander has the authority and responsibility to do the following for incidents within the Area Command:

- Provide agency or jurisdictional authority for assigned incidents.
- Ensure a clear understanding of agency expectations, intentions, and constraints.
- Establish critical resource use priorities between various incidents.
- Ensure that Incident Management Team personnel assignments and organizations are appropriate.
- Maintain contact with officials in charge, and other agencies and groups.
- Coordinate the demobilization or reassignment of resources between assigned incidents.

Multiagency Coordination Systems

Image 6.22

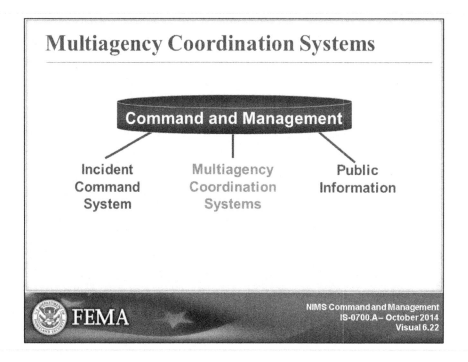

Key Points

- The second Command and Management element is the Multiagency Coordination Systems.
- Multiagency coordination is a process that allows all levels of government and all disciplines to work together more efficiently and effectively.
- The I-400 Advanced Incident Command System (ICS) course presents more detailed training on Multiagency Coordination Systems.

Image 6.23

Multiagency Coordination System (MACS)

A __system__ that provides the architecture to support:

- Coordination for incident prioritization,
- Critical resource allocation,
- Communications systems integration, and
- Information coordination.

FEMA

NIMS Command and Management
IS-0700.A – October 2014
Visual 6.23

Key Points

- NIMS describes MACS as providing "the architecture to support coordination for incident prioritization, critical resource allocation, communications systems integration, and information coordination. The elements of multiagency coordination systems include facilities, equipment, personnel, procedures, and communications."
- MACS functions typically include: situation assessment, incident priority determination, critical resource acquisition and allocation, support for relevant incident management policies and interagency activities, coordination with other MACS, and coordination of summary information.
- MACS assist agencies and organizations responding to an incident.
- The elements of a MACS include facilities, equipment, personnel, procedures, and communications.
- Two of the most commonly used elements are Emergency Operations Centers (EOCs) and Multiagency Coordination (MAC) Groups.

Common coordination elements may include:

- Dispatch Center
- EOC
- Department Operations Center (DOC)
- MAC Group

Image 6.24

Key Points

- In many emergencies, agencies have statutory responsibilities at incidents that extend beyond political jurisdictional boundaries. Many larger emergencies will involve two or more political subdivisions. It may be essential to establish a MACS to assist the coordination efforts on an area or regional basis.
- A MACS is not a physical location or facility. Rather, a MACS includes all components involved in managing events or incidents, and may include:
  - On-scene command structure and responders.
  - Resource coordination centers.
  - Coordination entities/groups.
  - Emergency Operations Centers.
  - Dispatch.

Image 6.25

Emergency Operations Center (EOC)

A central location that supports Incident Command by:

- Making executive/policy decisions.
- Coordinating interagency relations.
- Dispatching and tracking requested resources.
- Collecting, analyzing, and disseminating information.

The EOC does **not** command the on-scene level of the incident.

FEMA

NIMS Command and Management
IS-0700.A – October 2014
Visual 6.25

Key Points

An Emergency Operations Center (EOC) is a central location that supports Incident Command by:

- Making executive/policy decisions.
- Coordinating interagency relations.
- Dispatching and tracking requested resources.
- Collecting, analyzing, and disseminating information.

Image 6.26

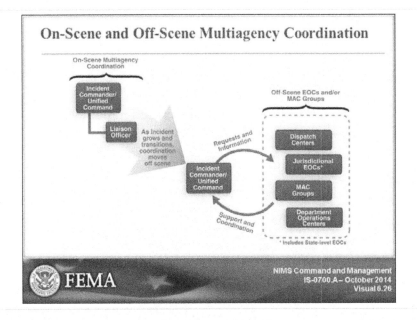

Key Points

Initially the Incident Command/Unified Command and the Liaison Officer may be able to provide all needed multiagency coordination at the scene. However, as the incident grows in size and complexity, offsite support and coordination may be required.

Coordination does not mean assuming command of the incident scene. Common coordination elements may include:

- **Dispatch Center:** A Dispatch Center coordinates the acquisition, mobilization, and movement of resources as ordered by the Incident Command/Unified Command.
- **Emergency Operations Center (EOC):** During an escalating incident, an EOC supports the on-scene response by relieving the burden of external coordination and securing additional resources. EOC core functions include coordination; communications; resource allocation and tracking; and information collection, analysis, and dissemination. EOCs may be staffed by personnel representing multiple jurisdictions and functional disciplines and a wide variety of resources.
- **Department Operations Center (DOC):** A DOC coordinates an internal agency incident management and response. A DOC is linked to and, in most cases, physically represented in the EOC by authorized agent(s) for the department or agency.
- **Multiagency Coordination (MAC) Group:** A MAC Group is comprised of administrators/executives, or their designees, who are authorized to represent or commit agency resources and funds. MAC Groups may also be known as multiagency committees or emergency management committees. A MAC Group does not have any direct incident involvement and will often be located some distance from the incident site(s) or may even function virtually. A MAC Group may require a support organization for its own logistics and documentation needs; to manage incident-related decision support information such as tracking critical resources, situation status, and intelligence or investigative information; and to provide public information to the news media and public. The number and skills of its personnel will vary by incident complexity, activity levels, needs of the MAC Group, and other factors identified through agreements or by preparedness organizations. A MAC Group may be established at any level (e.g., national, State, or local) or within any discipline (e.g., emergency management, public health, critical infrastructure, or private sector).

Image 6.27

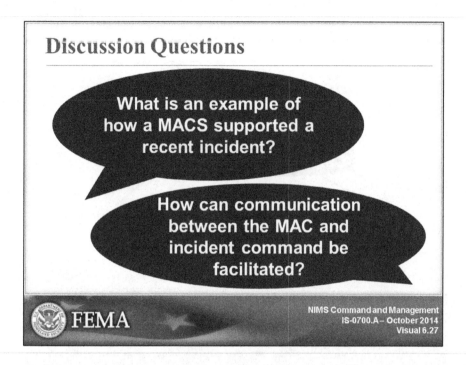

Key Points

Answer the following discussion questions:

- **What is an example of how a MACS supported a recent incident?**

- **How can communication between the MAC and Incident Command be facilitated?**

Public Information

Image 6.28

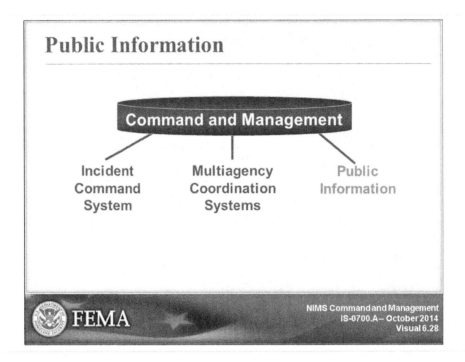

Key Points

The final Command and Management element is Public Information.

Image 6.29

Public Information

Public Information includes messages about:

- Lifesaving measures.
- Evacuation routes.
- Threat and alert system notices.
- Other public safety information.

FEMA

NIMS Command and Management
IS-0700.A – October 2014
Visual 6.29

Key Points

Public Information consists of the processes, procedures, and systems to communicate timely, accurate, and accessible information on the incident's cause, size, and current situation to the public, responders, and additional stakeholders (both directly affected and indirectly affected).

Public Information must be coordinated and integrated across jurisdictions, agencies, and organizations; among Federal, State, tribal, and local governments; and with nongovernmental organizations and the private sector.

Public Information, education strategies, and communications plans help ensure that numerous audiences receive timely, consistent messages about:

- Lifesaving measures.
- Evacuation routes.
- Threat and alert system notices.
- Other public safety information.

Image 6.30

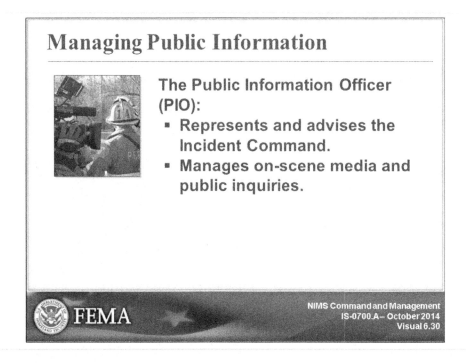

Key Points

- **Public information** consists of the processes, procedures, and systems to communicate timely, accurate, and accessible information on an incident's cause, size, and current situation to the public, responders, and additional stakeholders (both directly affected and indirectly affected). Public information must be coordinated and integrated across jurisdictions and agencies. Well-developed public information, education strategies, and communications plans help to ensure that lifesaving measures, evacuation routes, threat and alert systems, and other public safety information is coordinated and communicated to numerous audiences in a timely, consistent manner. Public information includes processes, procedures, and organizational structures required to gather, verify, coordinate, and disseminate information.
- The **Public Information Officer** (PIO) supports the Incident Command structure as a member of the Command staff. The PIO advises the Incident Commander on all public information matters relating to the management of the incident. The PIO handles inquiries from the media, the public, and elected officials; emergency public information and warnings; rumor monitoring and response; media monitoring; and other functions required to gather, verify, coordinate, and disseminate accurate, accessible, and timely information related to the incident, particularly regarding information on public health, safety, and protection.
- The PIO coordinates through the **Joint Information Center** (JIC), an interagency entity established to coordinate and disseminate information for the public and media concerning an incident. JICs may be established locally, regionally, or nationally depending on the size and magnitude of the incident.

Source: National Incident Management System

Image 6.31

Joint Information Center (JIC)

A JIC:

- May be established to coordinate public affairs functions.
- Serves as a focal point for coordinated and timely release of incident-related information to the public and the media.

FEMA

NIMS Command and Management
IS-0700.A – October 2014
Visual 6.31

Key Points

In order to coordinate the release of emergency information and other public affairs functions, a Joint Information Center (JIC) may be established.

The JIC is:

- A central location that facilitates operation of the Joint Information System.
- A location where personnel with public information responsibilities perform critical emergency information functions, crisis communications, and public affairs functions.

The JIC serves as a focal point for coordinated and timely release of incident-related information to the public and the media. Information about where to receive assistance is communicated directly to victims and their families in an accessible format and in appropriate languages for those with limited English proficiency.

JICs may be established at all levels of government, at incident sites, or can be components of Multiagency Coordination Systems (i.e., EOCs and the Joint Field Office).

A single JIC location is preferable, but the system is flexible and adaptable enough to accommodate virtual or multiple JIC locations, as required.

Image 6.32

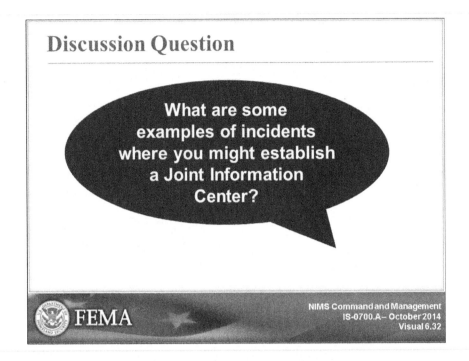

Key Points

Answer the following discussion question:

- **What are some examples of incidents where you might establish a Joint Information Center?**

Image 6.33

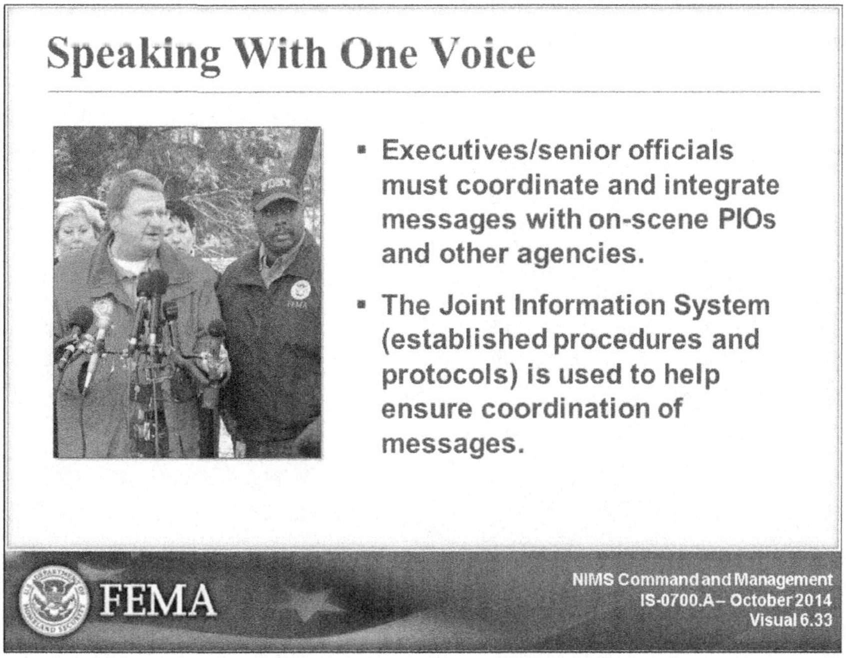

Speaking With One Voice

- Executives/senior officials must coordinate and integrate messages with on-scene PIOs and other agencies.
- The Joint Information System (established procedures and protocols) is used to help ensure coordination of messages.

FEMA

NIMS Command and Management
IS-0700.A – October 2014
Visual 6.33

Key Points

Executives/senior officials must coordinate and integrate messages with on-scene PIOs and other agencies.

The Joint Information System:

- Integrates incident information and public affairs into a cohesive organization designed to provide consistent, coordinated, timely information during crisis or incident operations.
- Provides a structure and system for:
- Develops and delivers coordinated interagency messages.
- Develops, recommends, and executes public information plans and strategies on behalf of the Incident Commander.
- Advises the Incident Commander concerning public affairs issues that could affect a response effort.
- Controls rumors and inaccurate information that could undermine public confidence in the emergency response effort.

The JIS is not a single physical location, but rather is a coordination framework that incorporates the on-scene Public Information Officer with other PIOs who may be located at the JIC, EOC, or other coordination center.

Image 6.34

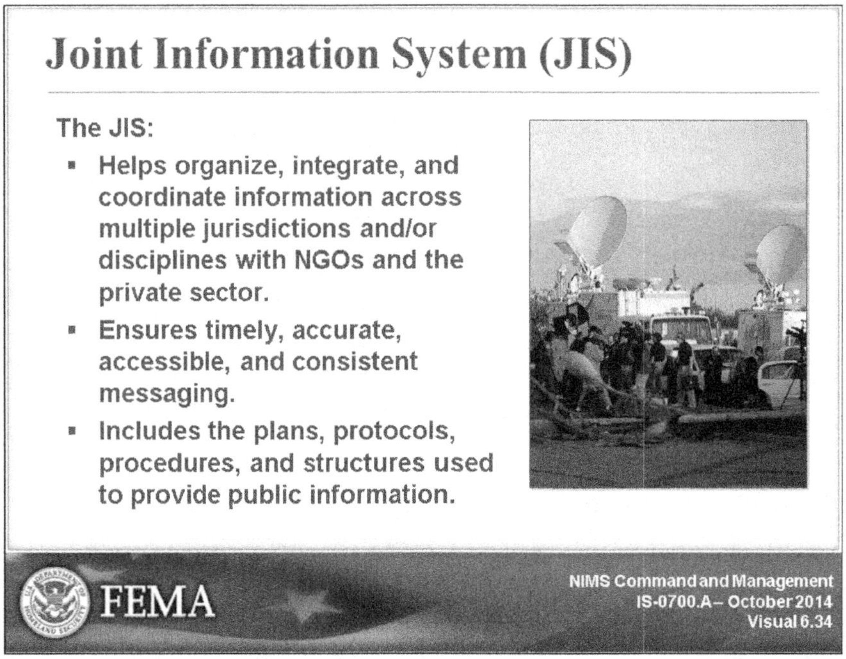

Joint Information System (JIS)

The JIS:

- Helps organize, integrate, and coordinate information across multiple jurisdictions and/or disciplines with NGOs and the private sector.
- Ensures timely, accurate, accessible, and consistent messaging.
- Includes the plans, protocols, procedures, and structures used to provide public information.

FEMA

NIMS Command and Management
IS-0700.A – October 2014
Visual 6.34

Key Points

The Joint Information System (JIS):

- Provides the mechanism to organize, integrate, and coordinate information to ensure timely, accurate, accessible, and consistent messaging across multiple jurisdictions and/or disciplines with nongovernmental organizations and the private sector.
- Includes the plans, protocols, procedures, and structures used to provide public information.

Federal, State, tribal, territorial, regional, or local PIOs and established JICs are critical supporting elements of the JIS.

Image 6.35

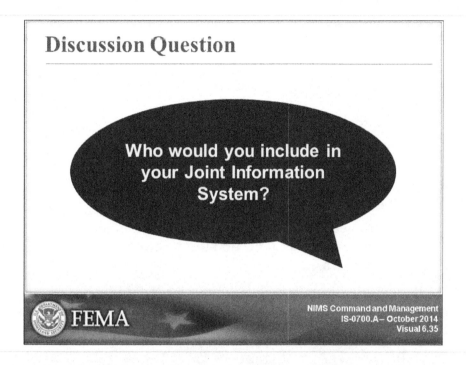

Key Points

Answer the following discussion question:

- **Who would you include in your Joint Information System?**

Knowledge Review and Summary

Image 6.36

Knowledge Review and Summary

Instructions:

- Answer the review questions on the next page in your Student Manual.
- Be prepared to share your answers with the class in 5 minutes.
- If you need clarification on any of the material presented in this unit, be sure to ask your instructors.

FEMA

NIMS Command and Management
IS-0700.A – October 2014
Visual 6.36

Key Points

Instructions:

- Answer the review questions on the next page.
- Be prepared to share your answers with the class in 5 minutes.
- If you need clarification on any of the material presented in this unit, ask your instructors.

Unit 6: Knowledge Review

1. What are the three elements within the NIMS Command and Management component?

2. Within NIMS, the act of directing, ordering, or controlling by virtue of explicit statutory, regulatory, or delegated authority at the field level is referred to as:

3. Reach each statement and then select the type of command being described.

	Type of Command		
	Single	Unified	Area
A natural gas pipeline broke and exploded into flames near a residential area. Officials representing law enforcement, public works, and fire/rescue are jointly managing the incident based on a single Incident Action Plan.	☐	☐	☐
Separate Incident Command organizations are directing the containment and cleanup of a widespread hazardous materials release. Each Incident Commander is responsible for a specified location and directly reports to a command organization that is managing across the incident sites.	☐	☐	☐
A lightning strike caused an abandoned warehouse to become engulfed in flames. A battalion chief has assumed command and is directing all operations including fire suppression and law enforcement perimeter control.	☐	☐	☐

4. Who is the individual responsible for all incident activities, including the development of strategies and tactics and the ordering and the release of resources?

5. Which position within the Command Staff interfaces with the public and media and/or with other agencies with incident-related information requirements?

6. Which position within the General Staff is responsible for the direct management of all incident-related tactical activities?

7. What is the name of the ICS document that establishes the overall incident objectives, strategies, and tactics?

8. Multiagency Coordination Systems (MACS) provide the architecture to support coordination for incident prioritization, critical resource allocation, communications systems integration, and information coordination. MACS assist agencies and organizations responding to an incident. MACS include facilities, equipment, personnel, procedures, and communications.

   Name an example of a MACS entity or element.

9. What is the name of the physical location at which the coordination of information and resources to support incident management (on-scene operations) activities normally takes place?

10. Review the actions below. Indicate if the action is consistent with NIMS Multiagency Coordination principles.

	Consistent with NIMS	Not Consistent with NIMS
A Planning Specialist at the Emergency Operations Center is establishing objectives and tactics for clearing a major traffic accident involving passenger vehicles and a gasoline tanker truck.	☐	☐
A water main break has disrupted the downtown area, and the on-scene Liaison Officer is working to coordinate the interface with the business owners.	☐	☐
A hurricane threat is requiring a mass evacuation of a county. The local Emergency Operations Center is coordinating with State officials on the timing of warnings/evacuation orders, traffic flow strategies, and staging of gasoline and other commodities along routes.	☐	☐

11. Which entity provides a structure for developing and delivering incident-related coordinated messages by developing, recommending, and executing public information plans and strategies?

12. What is the purpose of the Joint Information System?

13. User the space below to make note of any questions you have about the material covered in this unit.

Preparedness Self-Assessment

Image 6.37

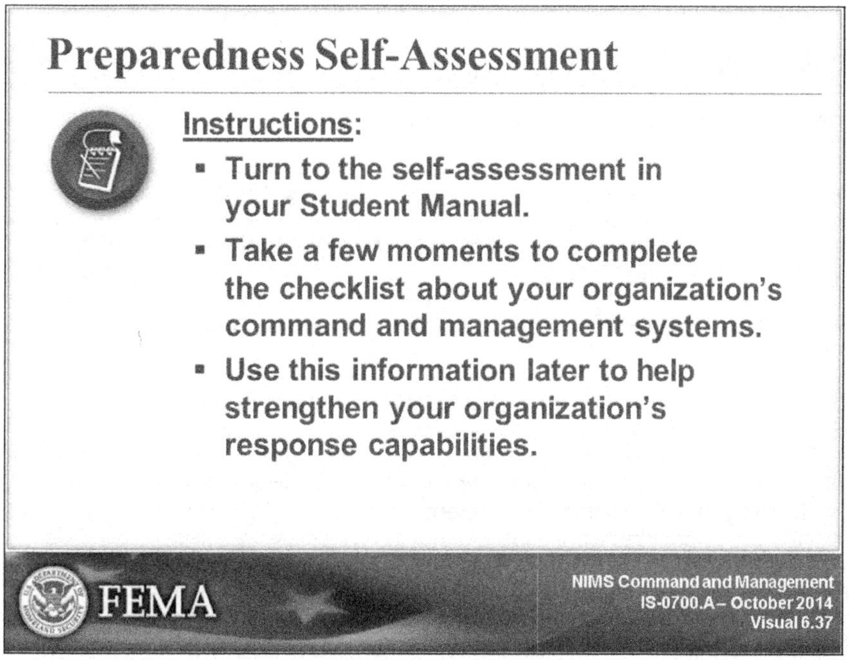

Preparedness Self-Assessment

Instructions:

- Turn to the self-assessment in your Student Manual.
- Take a few moments to complete the checklist about your organization's command and management systems.
- Use this information later to help strengthen your organization's response capabilities.

FEMA

NIMS Command and Management
IS-0700.A – October 2014
Visual 6.37

Key Points

Instructions:

- Turn to the self-assessments in your Student Manual.
- Take a few moments to complete the checklists about your organization's communications and information management systems.
- Use this information later to help strengthen your organization's response capabilities.

Self-Assessment: Command and Management Preparedness

Instructions: Complete the following self-assessment to assess your jurisdiction's, agency's, or organization's resource management systems preparedness. Use this information to ensure that your jurisdiction, agency, or organization is preparing effectively.

My jurisdiction, agency, or organization has	Yes	No
Emergency operations plans, policies, and procedures that are consistent with the NIMS principles.	☐	☐
Identified qualified personnel to assume ICS Command and General Staff positions.	☐	☐
Procedures for ensuring that common terminology is used for organizational functions, resource descriptions, and incident facilities.	☐	☐
Procedures for centralized, coordinated incident action planning to guide all response activities.	☐	☐
Conducted tabletop or functional exercises with all potential members of the Unified Command.	☐	☐
Procedures for addressing the interface between the on-scene Incident Command and other elements of the Multiagency Coordination System.	☐	☐
Conducted tabletop or functional exercises focusing on the interface between the on-scene Incident Command and other elements of the Multiagency Coordination System.	☐	☐
Processes and systems to communicate timely, accurate, and accessible information to the public.	☐	☐
Procedures for establishing a Joint Information Center.	☐	☐

Use the space below to make note of action items for your jurisdiction, agency, or organization.

Reference: Command and Management Features

The essential features are listed below:

Standardization:

- **Common Terminology:** Using common terminology helps to define organizational functions, incident facilities, resource descriptions, and position titles.

Command:

- **Establishment and Transfer of Command:** The command function must be clearly established from the beginning of an incident. When command is transferred, the process must include a briefing that captures all essential information for continuing safe and effective operations.
- **Chain of Command and Unity of Command:** Chain of command refers to the orderly line of authority within the ranks of the incident management organization. Unity of command means that every individual has a designated supervisor to whom he or she reports at the scene of the incident. These principles clarify reporting relationships and eliminate the confusion caused by multiple, conflicting directives. Incident managers at all levels must be able to control the actions of all personnel under their supervision.
- **Unified Command:** In incidents involving multiple jurisdictions, a single jurisdiction with multiagency involvement, or multiple jurisdictions with multiagency involvement, Unified Command allows agencies with different legal, geographic, and functional authorities and responsibilities to work together effectively without affecting individual agency authority, responsibility, or accountability.

Planning/Organizational Structure:

- **Management by Objectives:** Includes establishing overarching objectives; developing and issuing assignments, plans, procedures, and protocols; establishing specific, measurable objectives for various incident management functional activities; and directing efforts to attain the established objectives.
- **Modular Organization:** The Incident Command organizational structure develops in a top- down, modular fashion that is based on the size and complexity of the incident, as well as the specifics of the hazard environment created by the incident.
- **Incident Action Planning:** Incident Action Plans (IAPs) provide a coherent means of communicating the overall incident objectives in the contexts of both operational and support activities. Every incident must have an Incident Action Plan (IAP) that: (a) Specifies the incident objectives; (b) States the activities; (c) Covers a specified timeframe, called an operational period; (d) May be oral or written.
- **Manageable Span of Control:** Span of control is key to effective and efficient incident management. Within ICS, the span of control of any individual with incident management supervisory responsibility should range from three to seven subordinates.

Facilities and Resources:

- **Incident Locations and Facilities:** Various types of operational locations and support facilities are established in the vicinity of an incident to accomplish a variety of purposes. Typical predesignated facilities include Incident Command Posts, Bases, Camps, Staging Areas, Mass Casualty Triage Areas, and others as required.
- **Comprehensive Resource Management:** Resource management includes processes for categorizing, ordering, dispatching, tracking, and recovering resources. It also includes processes for reimbursement for resources, as appropriate. Resources are defined as personnel, teams, equipment, supplies, and facilities available or potentially available for assignment or allocation in support of incident

management and emergency response activities.

Communications/Information Management:

- **Integrated Communications:** Incident communications are facilitated through the development and use of a common communications plan and interoperable communications processes and architectures.
- **Information and Intelligence Management:** The incident management organization must establish a process for gathering, sharing, and managing incident-related information and intelligence.

Professionalism:

- **Accountability:** Effective accountability at all jurisdictional levels and within individual functional areas during incident operations is essential. To that end, the following principles must be adhered to:
    - **Check-In:** All responders, regardless of agency affiliation, must report in to receive an assignment in accordance with the procedures established by the Incident Commander.
    - **Incident Action Plan:** Response operations must be directed and coordinated as outlined in the IAP.
    - **Unity of Command:** Each individual involved in incident operations will be assigned to only one supervisor.
    - **Span of Control:** Supervisors must be able to adequately supervise and control their subordinates, as well as communicate with and manage all resources under their supervision.
    - **Resource Tracking:** Supervisors must record and report resource status changes as they occur. (This topic is covered in a later unit.)
- **Dispatch/Deployment:** Personnel and equipment should respond only when requested or when dispatched by an appropriate authority.

Reference: Command Staff

Position	Responsibilities
Public Information Officer	The Public Information Officer is responsible for interfacing with the public and media and/or with other agencies with incident-related information requirements. The Public Information Officer gathers, verifies, coordinates, and disseminates accurate, accessible, and timely information on the incident's cause, size, and current situation; resources committed; and other matters of general interest for both internal and external audiences.
	The Public Information Officer may also perform a key public information- monitoring role. Whether the command structure is single or unified, only one Public Information Officer should be designated per incident. Assistants may be assigned from other involved agencies, departments, or organizations. The Incident Commander/Unified Command must approve the release of all incident-related information.
	In large-scale incidents or where multiple command posts are established, the Public Information Officer should participate in or lead the Joint Information Center in order to ensure consistency in the provision of information to the public.
Safety Officer	The Safety Officer monitors incident operations and advises the Incident Commander/Unified Command on all matters relating to operational safety, including the health and safety of emergency responder personnel. The ultimate responsibility for the safe conduct of incident management operations rests with the Incident Commander/Unified Command and
	supervisors at all levels of incident management.
	The Safety Officer is, in turn, responsible to the Incident Commander/Unified

Position	Responsibilities
	Command for the systems and procedures necessary to ensure ongoing assessment of hazardous environments, including the incident Safety Plan, coordination of multiagency safety efforts, and implementation of measures to promote emergency responder safety, as well as the general safety of incident operations. The Safety Officer has immediate authority to stop and/or prevent unsafe acts during incident operations.
	It is important to note that the agencies, organizations, or jurisdictions that contribute to joint safety management efforts do not lose their individual identities or responsibility for their own programs, policies, and personnel. Rather, each contributes to the overall effort to protect all responder personnel involved in incident operations.
Liaison Officer	The Liaison Officer is Incident Command's point of contact for representatives of other governmental agencies, nongovernmental organizations, and the private sector (with no jurisdiction or legal authority) to provide input on their agency's policies, resource availability, and other incident-related matters.
	Under either a single Incident Commander or a Unified Command structure, representatives from assisting or cooperating agencies and organizations coordinate through the Liaison Officer.
	Agency and organizational representatives assigned to an incident must have the authority to speak for their parent agencies or organizations on all matters, following appropriate consultations with their agency leadership.
	Assistants and personnel from other agencies or organizations (public or private) involved in incident management activities may be assigned to the Liaison Officer to facilitate coordination.
Technical Specialists	Technical specialists can be used to fill other or additional Command Staff positions required based on the nature and location(s) of the incident or specific requirements established by Incident Command.
	For example, a legal counsel might be assigned to the Planning Section as a technical specialist or directly to the Command Staff to advise Incident Command on legal matters, such as emergency proclamations, the legality of evacuation orders, and legal rights and restrictions pertaining to media access.
	Similarly, a medical advisor—an agency operational medical director or assigned physician—might be designated to provide advice and recommendations to Incident Command about medical and mental health services, mass casualty, acute care, vector control, epidemiology, or mass prophylaxis considerations, particularly in the response to a bioterrorism incident.
	In addition, a Special Needs Advisor might be designated to provide expertise regarding communication, transportation, supervision, and essential services for diverse populations in the affected area.

Reference: General Staff

Position	Responsibilities
Operations	The Operations Section is responsible for all tactical activities focused on reducing the immediate hazard, saving lives and property, establishing situational control, and restoring normal operations. Lifesaving and responder safety will always be the highest priorities and the first objectives in the Incident Action Plan.
	Expansions of this basic structure may vary according to numerous considerations and operational factors. In some cases, a strictly functional approach may be used. In other cases, the organizational structure will be determined by

Position	Responsibilities
	geographical/jurisdictional boundaries. In still others, a mix of functional and geographical considerations may be appropriate. The ICS offers flexibility in determining the right structural approach for the specific circumstances of the incident at hand.
	Operations Section Chief: The Section Chief is responsible to Incident Command for the direct management of all incident-related tactical activities. The Operations Section Chief will establish tactics for the assigned operational period. An Operations Section Chief should be designated for each operational period, and responsibilities include direct involvement in development of the Incident Action Plan.
	Branches: Branches may serve several purposes and may be functional, geographic, or both, depending on the circumstances of the incident. In general, Branches are established when the number of Divisions or Groups exceeds the recommended span of control. Branches are identified by the use of Roman numerals or by functional area.
	Divisions and Groups: Divisions and/or Groups are established when the number of resources exceeds the manageable span of control of Incident Command and the Operations Section Chief. Divisions are established to divide an incident into physical or geographical areas of operation. Groups are established to divide the incident into functional areas of operation. For certain types of incidents, for example, Incident Command may assign evacuation or mass care responsibilities to a functional group in the Operations Section. Additional levels of supervision may also exist below the Division or Group level.
	Resources: Resources may be organized and managed in three different ways, depending on the requirements of the incident: • **Single Resources:** These are individual personnel, supplies, or equipment and any associated operators. • **Task Forces:** These are any combination of resources assembled in support of a specific mission or operational need. All resource elements within a Task Force must have common communications and a designated leader. • **Strike Teams:** These are a set number of resources of the same kind and type that have an established minimum number of personnel. All resource elements within a Strike Team must have common communications and a designated leader. The use of Task Forces and Strike Teams is encouraged wherever possible to optimize the use of resources, reduce the span of control over a large number of single resources, and reduce the complexity of incident management coordination and communications.
Planning	The Planning Section collects, evaluates, and disseminates incident situation information and intelligence for the Incident Commander/Unified Command and incident management personnel. This Section then prepares status reports, displays situation information, maintains the status of resources assigned to the incident, and prepares and documents the Incident Action Plan, based on Operations Section input and guidance from the Incident Commander/Unified Command. The Planning Section is comprised of four primary units, as well as a number of technical specialists to assist in evaluating the situation, developing planning options, and forecasting requirements for additional resources. These primary units that fulfill functional requirements are: • **Resources Unit:** Responsible for recording the status of resources committed to the incident. This unit also evaluates resources committed currently to the incident, the effects additional responding resources will have on the incident, and anticipated resource needs.

Position	Responsibilities
	• **Situation Unit:** Responsible for the collection, organization, and analysis of incident status information, and for analysis of the situation as it progresses. • **Demobilization Unit:** Responsible for ensuring orderly, safe, and efficient demobilization of incident resources. • **Documentation Unit:** Responsible for collecting, recording, and safeguarding all documents relevant to the incident. • **Technical Specialist(s):** Personnel with special skills that can be used anywhere within the ICS organization. The Planning Section is normally responsible for gathering and disseminating information and intelligence critical to the incident, unless the Incident Commander/Unified Command places this function elsewhere. The Planning Section is also responsible for assembling and documenting the Incident Action Plan. The Incident Action Plan includes the overall incident objectives and strategies established by Incident Command. In the case of Unified Command, the Incident Action Plan must adequately address the mission and policy needs of each jurisdictional agency, as well as interaction between jurisdictions, functional agencies, and private organizations. The Incident Action Plan also addresses tactics and support activities required for one operational period, generally 12 to 24 hours. The Incident Action Plan should incorporate changes in strategies and tactics based on lessons learned during earlier operational periods. A written Incident Action Plan is especially important when: resources from multiple agencies and/or jurisdictions are involved, the incident will span several operational periods; changes in shifts of personnel and/or equipment are required, or there is a need to document actions and decisions.
Logistics	The Logistics Section is responsible for all service support requirements needed to facilitate effective and efficient incident management, including ordering resources from off-incident locations. This Section also provides facilities, security (of the Incident Command facilities), transportation, supplies, equipment maintenance and fuel, food services, communications and information technology support, and emergency responder medical services, including inoculations, as required. The Logistics Section is led by a Section Chief, who may also have one or more deputies. Having a deputy is encouraged when all designated units are established at an incident site. When the incident is very large or requires a number of facilities with large numbers of equipment, the Logistics Section can be divided into two Branches. This helps with span of control by providing more effective supervision and coordination among the individual units. Conversely, in smaller incidents or when fewer resources are needed, a Branch configuration may be used to combine the task assignments of individual units. The Logistics Section has six primary units that fulfill the functional requirements: • **Supply Unit:** Orders, receives, stores, and processes all incident related resources, personnel, and supplies. • **Ground Support Unit:** Provides all ground transportation during an incident. In conjunction with providing transportation, the unit is also responsible for maintaining and supplying vehicles, keeping usage records, and developing incident traffic plans. • **Facilities Unit:** Sets up, maintains, and demobilizes all facilities used in support of incident operations. The unit also provides facility maintenance and security services required to support incident operations. • **Food Unit:** Determines food and water requirements, plans menus, orders food, provides cooking facilities, cooks, serves, maintains food service areas,

Position	Responsibilities
	and manages food security and safety concerns. • **Communications Unit:** Major responsibilities include effective communications planning as well as acquiring, setting up, maintaining, and accounting for communications equipment. • **Medical Unit:** Responsible for the effective and efficient provision of medical services to incident personnel.
Finance/ Administration	A Finance/Administration Section is established when the incident management activities require on-scene or incident-specific finance and other administrative support services. Some of the functions that fall within the scope of this Section are recording personnel time, maintaining vendor contracts, compensation and claims, and conducting an overall cost analysis for the incident. If a separate Finance/Administration Section is established, close coordination with the Planning Section and Logistics Section is also essential so that operational records can be reconciled with financial documents. The Finance/Administration Section is a critical part of ICS in large, complex incidents involving significant funding originating from multiple sources. In addition to monitoring multiple sources of funds, the Section Chief must track and report to Incident Command the accrued cost as the incident progresses. This allows the Incident Commander/Unified Command to forecast the need for additional funds before operations are negatively affected. Within the Finance/Administration Section, four primary units fulfill functional requirements: • **Compensation/Claims Unit:** Responsible for financial concerns resulting from property damage, injuries, or fatalities at the incident. • **Cost Unit:** Responsible for tracking costs, analyzing cost data, making estimates, and recommending cost-saving measures. • **Procurement Unit:** Responsible for financial matters concerning vendor contracts. • **Time Unit:** Responsible for recording time for incident personnel and hired equipment.

UNIT 7: ADDITIONAL RESOURCES AND COURSE SUMMARY

Objectives

At the end of this unit, you should be able to:

- Describe the role of the National Integration Center.
- Identify the role of supporting technologies in NIMS implementation.
- Take the final exam.

Scope

- Unit Introduction and Objectives
- National Integration Center
- NIC Responsibilities
- NIMS Resource Center
- Taking the Exam
- Feedback

Unit Introduction and Objectives

Image 7.1

Key Points

Unit 7 summarizes the course material and describes additional resources that are available. The next visual will outline the objectives for this unit.

Image 7.2

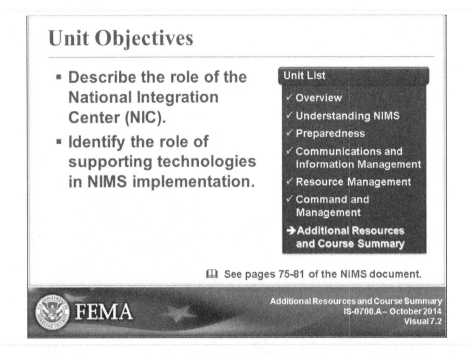

Key Points

This lesson presents information about the ongoing management and maintenance of the National Incident Management System (NIMS).

At the completion of this lesson, you should be able to:

- Describe the role of the National Integration Center.
- Identify the role of supporting technologies in NIMS implementation.

This lesson summarizes the information presented in Component V: Ongoing Management and Maintenance, including:

- National Integration Center
- Supporting Technologies

Refer to pages 75 through 81 of the NIMS document.

National Integration Center

Image 7.3

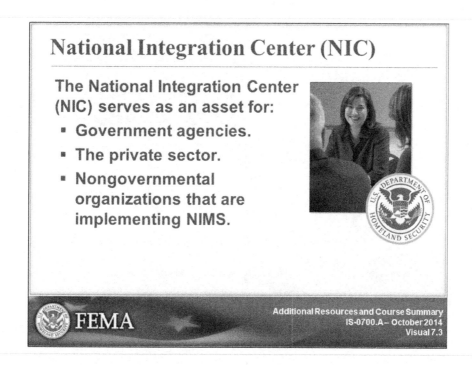

Key Points

HSPD-5 required the Secretary of Homeland Security to establish a mechanism for ensuring the ongoing management and maintenance of NIMS.

The Secretary established the National Integration Center (NIC) to serve as an asset for government agencies, the private sector, and nongovernmental organizations that are implementing NIMS.

Image 7.4

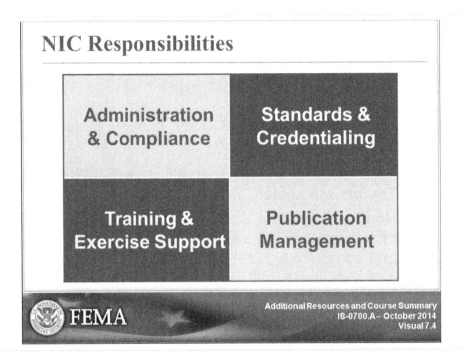

Key Points

The NIC is responsible for the following functions:

- **Administration and Compliance:** To manage ongoing administration and implementation of NIMS, including specification of compliance measures, the NIC is responsible for working toward the following:
    - Developing and maintaining a national program for NIMS education and awareness.
    - Promoting compatibility between national-level standards for NIMS and those developed by other public, private, and professional groups.
    - Facilitating the establishment and maintenance of a documentation and database system related to qualification, certification, and credentialing of emergency management/response personnel and organizations.
    - Developing assessment criteria for the various components of NIMS, as well as compliance requirements and timelines.
- **Standards and Credentialing:** The NIC will work with appropriate standards development organizations to ensure the adoption of common national standards and credentialing systems that are compatible and aligned with the implementation of NIMS. The standards apply to the identification, adoption, and development of common standards and credentialing programs.
- **Training and Exercise Support:** To lead the development of training and exercises that further appropriate agencies' and organizations' knowledge, adoption, and implementation of NIMS, the NIC will coordinate with them to do the following:
    - Facilitate the definition of general training requirements and the development of national-level training standards and course curricula associated with NIMS.
    - Facilitate the development of national standards, guidelines, and protocols for incident management training and exercises, including consideration of existing exercise and training programs at all jurisdictional levels.
    - Facilitate the development of training necessary to support the incorporation of NIMS across all jurisdictional levels.

- o Establish and maintain a repository for reports and lessons learned from actual incidents, training, and exercises, as well as for best practices, model structures, and processes for NIMS-related functions.
- **Publication Management:** Publication management for NIMS includes the development of naming and numbering conventions, the review and certification of publications, development of methods for publications control, identification of sources and suppliers for publications and related services, management of publication distribution, and assurance of product accessibility.

Image 7.5

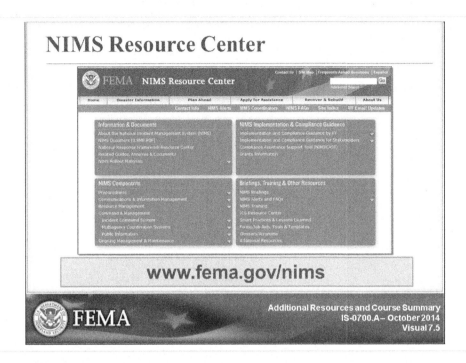

Key Points

Refer to the NIMS Resource Center, www.fema.gov/NIMS for more information, additional reference materials, related training, and links to other resources.

Exam

Image 7.6

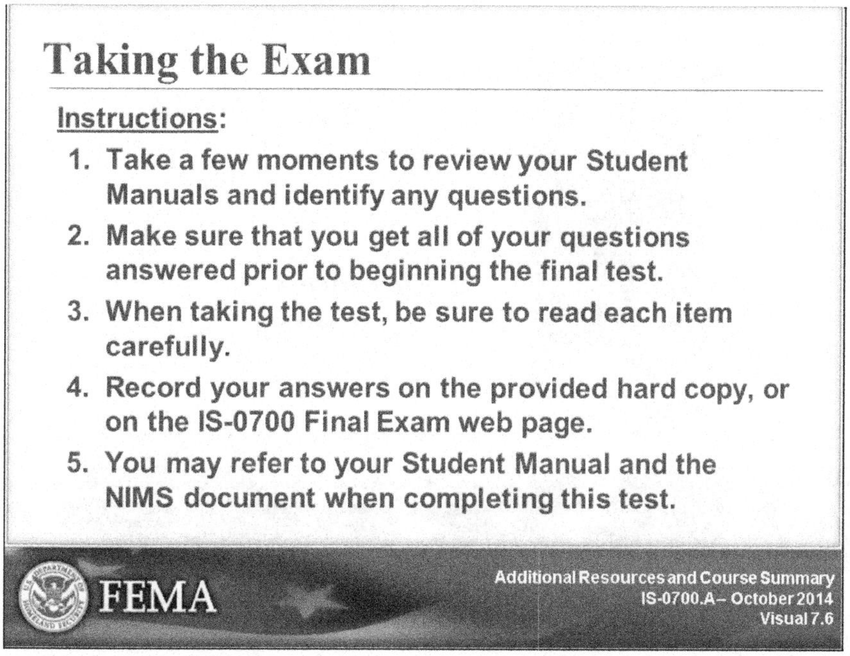

Taking the Exam

Instructions:

1. Take a few moments to review your Student Manuals and identify any questions.
2. Make sure that you get all of your questions answered prior to beginning the final test.
3. When taking the test, be sure to read each item carefully.
4. Record your answers on the provided hard copy, or on the IS-0700 Final Exam web page.
5. You may refer to your Student Manual and the NIMS document when completing this test.

Additional Resources and Course Summary
IS-0700.A – October 2014
Visual 7.6

Key Points

Instructions:

- Take a few moments to review your Student Manuals and identify any questions.
- Make sure that you get all of your questions answered prior to beginning the final test.
- When taking the test be sure to read each item carefully.
- Record your answers on the provided hard copy, or on the IS-700 Final Exam web page.
- You may refer to your Student Manual and the NIMS document when completing this test.

Image 7.7

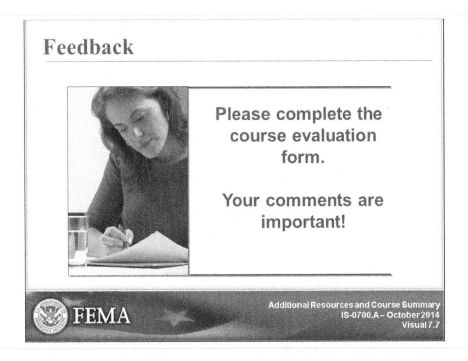

Key Points

Completing the course evaluation form is important. Your comments will be used to evaluate the effectiveness of this course and make changes for future versions.